How to Go to "CAMP"

How to Go to "CAMP"

Surviving in a Women's Federal Prison

By
V. Cheryl Womack

DEDICATION

To my husband, Dean, whose unwavering support and
love helped me survive the darkest times of my life.
To my sons Andrew and Ryan, you make me
strive to be a better person, mother, and friend.

Published by;
Tremendous Leadership
PO Box 267 • Boiling Springs, PA 17007
(717) 701 - 8159 • (800) 233 - 2665
www.TremendousLeadership.com

Published Work © 2024 Women of Worth not for
profit 501(c3) Text © 2024 V. Cheryl Womack

Managing Editor - Dr. Tracey C. Jones
Copy Editors - V. Cheryl Womack, Katrina H McLarin
Cover Design – Tim Schulte

Paperback ISBN 979-8-9920254-0-8
eBook ISBN 979-8-9920254-1-5

DESIGNED & PRINTED IN THE UNITED STATES OF AMERICA

LIST OF ACRONYMS

A&O	Admissions & Orientation
BOP	Federal Bureau of Prisons
CE	Continuing Education
CO	Correctional Officer
CORRLINKS	Email system used by BOP to allow inmates to communicate to the outside world
FCI	Federal Correctional Institution
FPC	Federal Prison Camp (Camp)
GED	General Equivalency Diploma
MP3	MPEG Audio Layer III - player
PA	Public Announcement
PAC	Phone Access Code
PIN	Commissary Personal Identification Number
PRN	Latin phrase "pro re nata," which means "as the need arises" nurse
RDAP	Residential Drug Abuse Program
RRCs	Residential Reentry Centers (Halfway Houses)
SHU	Special Housing Unit, a type of prison cell used to isolate inmates

TRUFONE Inmate Telephone System

TRULINCS The Trust Fund Limited Inmate
Computer System

LIST OF TERMINOLOGY

10 Minute Walk	Top of each hour, time allowed to get from one destination to the next
Body Search	Correctional Officer body search of an inmate
Bunk Pass	For over 60 or medically disabled
Bus Stop	Temporary group lodging
Call-out Sheet	A daily sheet in alphabetical order showing inmate appointments per dorm
Camp	Federal Prison Camp
Case Manager	Works with the BOP to help women transition to the next phase of reentry
Co-defendants	Multiple participants for the same crime
Contraband	Anything in your possession not supported by the original proof of purchase
Cop-out	Communication form between the inmate and prison administration
Good Time	A 15% reduction in the time served based on good behavior
Halfway House	A place where people who have recently left a prison, mental hospital, etc., can live until they are considered ready to live by themselves

Lockdown	When inmates are confined to a room or dorm
Mail Call	Distribution of inmate mail
On The Books	Inmate funds in TRULINCS
Outstanding Warrants	A judge has issued an arrest warrant
Pill-call	Medication distribution for pills or insulin
Probation	Time served after your prison sentence
Recall	30 minutes before any count everyone must be off campus and in their room
Shakedown	An inmate, group or dorm could have a surprise inspection
Shot	A rule violation write-up
Side Hustle	Generating illegal credit for services or goods
Special Order	Big ticket items outside of commissary; tennis shoes, crafts, and religious items

CONTENTS

Chapter One

FALL FROM GRACE

Let me start this book by sharing with you my story and perspective on how things work in a Federal Prison Camp. I learned so much and will forever appreciate the friendships and help I had from the other women while incarcerated. Some of you may have your own experiences, and I value your take, but here, I can only offer my perspective from the experience I lived.

In the early 2000s, I was at the height of my career, known as one of the most influential female entrepreneurs and philanthropists in Kansas City. My name was recognized, not just locally but on a broader stage. I had sold my businesses, invested in others' dreams, and was deeply involved in mentoring through the prestigious Committee of 200.

My career in the trucking insurance industry had been demanding but rewarding. I wasn't just an insurance broker but an advocate for independent truckers across the United States, many of whom relied on me to navigate the complex regulations that threatened their livelihoods. I testified before the IRS in Washington, D.C., and my association for independent truckers grew steadily, with thousands of members who saw me as their champion.

However, when I sold my business, I found myself in unfamiliar territory. The transition was challenging. The thrill of my new ventures soon turned into a difficult-to-manage whirlwind. I had been advised to take time to adjust to major life changes, but I ignored that advice, diving headfirst into a chaotic mix of new projects, investments, and responsibilities. In my haste, I made mistakes and errors in judgement that would eventually lead to my downfall.

As I embarked on these new ventures, I delegated responsibilities to others, trusting them to manage my finances and business affairs. This trust, however, was misplaced. Oversight was lacking, and I ignored warning signs that something was amiss. The severe consequences led to a situation that spiraled out of control.

I was blindsided when I discovered the extent of the financial mismanagement that had occurred under my watch. I took my eye off the ball, and a staff member stole over $3 million! The investigation into that crime led to my eventual indictment, which cost me over $15 million in legal, accounting, and miscellaneous fees. My once-thriving business empire was now in jeopardy, and I faced legal challenges that would consume the next nine years of my life. This story will fill another book. Turning over these businesses' financial management is one of my life's greatest mistakes, and I'm still paying for these decisions. Despite my best efforts, I found myself entangled in a legal battle that ultimately resulted in my imprisonment. I endured the hardship of serving 15 out of 18 months in a Women's Federal Prison Camp.

Looking back, I realize that my story is not unique. Many successful individuals are caught in the storm of their own success, unaware of the dangers lurking beneath the surface. The lessons I've learned from this experience are invaluable, and I am committed to sharing them with others who may find themselves in similar situations.

Maybe you, too, trusted the wrong person, developed a destructive habit, or had a complete lapse in judgment. Whatever brought you to this point, it's time to focus on what's to come. The past is the past, and while it's important to learn from it, what matters now is how you prepare for the future. The key is to recognize the blind spot behaviors and decisions that led you here and ensure they don't define your future.

I understand the fear, uncertainty, and stress that come with facing the possibility, and reality, of imprisonment. I've been there, and I've lived through the consequences of my actions. But I also know that it's possible to rebuild, to learn from mistakes, and to use those experiences to help others. My journey has been challenging but has also given me a unique perspective and the strength to guide others through difficult times.

This book is not just a recounting of my fall from grace; it's a testament to resilience, recovery, and the power of second chances. I want to help others prepare for the challenges ahead, face them with courage, and emerge stronger on the other side. Because if there's one thing I've learned, it's that no matter how far you fall, it's possible to rise again.

Chapter Two
GET IT TOGETHER

This book focuses on Women's Prison Camps. While the preparation and knowledge needed are similar for most types of incarceration, this book does not specifically address the details of being placed in a higher-security prison.

What facts do you need right now—before, during, and after your imprisonment? The issues facing women behind bars often differ from those men deal with in many instances. I know you are overwhelmed and unsure where to begin or what to do. This book intends to provide much-needed information and helpful tips for you and your family.

It's a scary time, from the moment you are indicted through to sentencing, it can feel paralyzing. The fear of the unknown for you and your family is daunting, making it hard to stay focused under these circumstances. Your first opportunity to self-surrender, as opposed to being arrested and brought in, is once you are indicted. You have been arrested and booked, or you are permitted to turn yourself in. When you self-surrender, you should wear no jewelry except a plain wedding band. They will take your picture, fingerprint you, review factual details about your life, and may hold you until it's time to go to court for your bail hearing.

If you have a passport, they will take it from you now. I was fortunate enough to wait around the courthouse until the hearing and appear in person with my attorney. You might be brought in shackled from the cell directly for sentencing. This hearing is about how you will spend your time between now and the actual trial. I was released on my own recognizance (that means I did not post bail as I was not considered a flight risk).

If you have to post bail, you will need to see a bondsman to determine what cash you need to come up with for them to post bail for you. It could take your family some time for this process, and you would have to remain incarcerated until the funding is met. You will also be assigned a Federal Probation Officer who you will meet that day. They will ask you questions about your life and your situation, and they will take lots of notes. They will be coming to your living quarters to determine if it is suitable to remain there during this time.

If you have not been held on remand, this is the second time you might be able to self-surrender. At sentencing, you may feel like you've just been told you have six months to live—that's precisely how I felt at that moment. I needed a second set of ears to help me process as I was in shock and not taking everything in. Your loved ones are also figuring out how to cope with your absence, no matter how long it may be. Shame and guilt may rear their ugly heads paralyzing you. These feelings can act as weapons that can stop you from doing anything. It provides cover for secrecy that strips away any control you might have. From the beginning of sentencing, you need to do the necessary work in a very short period.

Once sentenced, the judicial system is figuring out if you need to wear an ankle monitor or not, if where you live is suitable during this timeframe, or if you need to make other arrangements they deem needed. They will visit you randomly wherever you live to ensure you follow the rules while you are out on bail. You will also have to check in by phone at a scheduled time each week. If you are out of jail, following all rules to the tee is essential to ensure you remain out. This reality is your life between now and prison. Between sentencing and self-surrender, you will receive an email, phone call, or letter from the Bureau of Prisons (BOP) telling you where you are going and what time to be there. Your letter, phone call, or email will contain all the details of where you have been designated to serve your time, including your specific date and time to arrive.

You must approach this experience as if you are going somewhere for serious medical treatments. I wanted to know everything about what was about to happen. Where are you going, and what is it like there? Is this the safest or closest facility, and do you have choices? Once you have found—through research and hopefully with the help of your attorney—the best or nearest location for you, insist that your attorney put that request in a letter to your judge. The judge is not required to honor this request but often considers it. This approval could help you be closer to your family, making visits easier. The BOP makes the ultimate decision but can be influenced by a judge's recommendation. Don't let anyone tell you otherwise—you can have some influence over where you are going.

To feel we had some control over the situation, my family and I came up with a safe word that I would use if I ever felt in danger and couldn't express it openly. It's much like what we did for our children when they were young or might do for our parents in elder care. It provided a way to share concerns if something terrible happened. We never needed it, but it gave us all peace of mind, especially my two adult sons. I strongly recommend establishing a safe word; it can make a significant difference.

To have any control over the situation the easiest way to arrive at a Camp is to self-surrender. You should push your attorney to confirm that you can do this. If given this opportunity, consider yourself fortunate. Although you may not see it now, this is a blessing. If you have to go to prison, self-surrender is the preferred way to get there. I realize how difficult it is to have a family member or friend deliver you to Camp—it is emotionally unfathomable—but somehow, you will find the strength to do it.

Make no mistake—this is not a hotel with a suggested check-in time. Being at the Camp **on time** is of utmost importance, whether it requires a bus, train, plane, Uber, or even hitchhiking. They don't care how you get there—just **get there**. If something unexpected happens and you have a reasonable explanation for not being able to self-surrender by your designated time, there is a phone number on the Department of Justice letter to call. If you do not self-surrender and do not call, be assured that the U.S. Marshals will issue a warrant for your arrest, and they **will** come looking for you. They **will** find you.

As a caregiver, provider, mother, and daughter, you have many roles to fill in your absence. You need to identify who will be in charge of each of these responsibilities while you are away. I found it helpful to divide my responsibilities among a few different people. Links to some of the legal forms needed are provided at the back of this book.

The government could freeze your bank account if you owe restitution at any time during this process, so your family's cash flow might need to run through other family members' accounts. Who will that person be? Visit your bank in person and explain your plans; this can go a long way toward stabilizing these situations. Do the same with your attorneys, accountants, bankers, insurance companies, pastor, employer, and your kids' school. Sometimes, you don't have anyone to help; these non-family connections can make all the difference in the world.

Before you go to Camp it's time to make a physical list of names, complete addresses, and phone numbers for anyone you may need to contact. Go through your phone and list all the important contacts, including family members and friends. Keep these numbers on a piece of paper that you store in your locker while you are at Camp. Maintain one folder labeled "Personal Information" separate from any other paperwork.

You can add up to 100 contacts to your approved list for emailing, calling, or scheduling video chats. When you add them, you will specify the type of communication permitted for each contact. For some, it might be phone calls; for others, emails or mailing addresses for sending letters. You should first add your Camp's complete mailing address, including your Camp ID at the top before your name. Some Camps are strict about using labels for mailing and require your ID number and return address on everything.

Ensure your entire list of essential contacts is complete. You never know when you might need to make an emergency call or send an urgent email. When situations arise, having everything in place allows you to deal with them more effectively. Here is a suggested list of information that might be useful:

- Your attorney's contact information
- Bank information, including all account numbers
- Insurance providers and policy numbers
- Mortgage company information and account number
- Kids' school contact information
- Pastors or spiritual advisors
- Elderly parents' care facilities
- Medication lists with dosages

Do you have your kids' doctors' numbers? Is there a babysitter? Add anyone you might need to reach. Go through your phone and compile this list, including complete addresses, as you may be writing to them. You will likely write more while you are away because emails and phone time cost money, and budgets can be tight. Even if you have enough money, the Camp has its own budgets that you will need to follow.

Consider making a list of all your passwords for various accounts and devices. Be cautious about who you share this information with, but providing it to trusted individuals can be very helpful. Consider using a Power of Attorney. Remember, you will have no access to the internet at Camp. You can change all your passwords when you return, and this handy list will help you recall what needs to be updated. Remember to make arrangements for your pets as well.

If you have legal documents, you should place them in a safe deposit box if you have nowhere else to store them. If you keep a calendar of any type, transfer that information into a written planner covering the time you will be away. You can provide different information to the various people helping you manage aspects of your life. Creating one comprehensive calendar and bringing it with you can help maintain your sanity and serve as a reminder for others.

Who will be caring for your minor children? Often, there is pressure to give up all rights to your young children, but you do not have to agree to this. Many women make hasty decisions under stress and later struggle to regain visitation rights after release. Try to work out an agreement for visits. Don't let shame stand in the way of a lifelong relationship with your children. This, too, shall pass. Don't do things you will regret later because you felt guilty. Take a deep breath and be the mother you know you can be by making proper plans for your children.

Will your children stay in the same school or attend a different one depending on who they live with? Does the calendar include their annual medical check-ups for school? Where are their immunization records? Who is managing these tasks, and do they have the necessary information to provide proof of any required vaccinations? If possible, visit the new school and meet with the principal to establish contact. Bring that information with you.

If you rely on Social Security, be aware that your benefits will stop when you go to Camp and will not start until after your release from the BOP system, including your time in a halfway house (RRCs). If this is a key source of your income, you need to plan accordingly. Your Medicare benefits will also be affected. Although your medical care is provided through the BOP until the day you are released, your Medicare coverage will not resume until 30 days **after** you are out of the BOP system, and coverage starts on the first of the following month.

Example: I continued paying for Medicare to avoid reduced benefits later. I was released from the BOP on December 19th. Despite paying, my Medicare coverage did not resume until February 1st. I had no healthcare coverage from December 19th to February 1st. For anyone, this is not a good situation; for an older person, it is terrifying. Having a gap in any benefit is something I had to learn through personal experience. I don't think anyone realizes or cares until it happens to them.

Before you go to Camp, use this time to prioritize your health and well-being. Schedule a doctor's appointment for a check-up, and ensure your medications are accurate and up-to-date. Make an appointment with your dentist, and if you're due for a breast exam, take care of it before you leave. Visit your gynecologist as well. In the midst of managing everything else, it's crucial to tend to your own essential health needs.

While this is time-consuming and a lot of work, you will be thankful every day you are away for taking the time to sort through all of this. Remember, preparation is key to maintaining as much normalcy and control as possible during this challenging time. These steps will help ensure that you and your loved ones are better equipped to handle the road ahead.

Chapter Three

IF YOU OWN IT, SELL IT

While away at Camp, you face the challenge of what to do with your possessions when sentenced to prison. Whether it's a car, a home, or other things of value, making arrangements to safeguard these possessions is crucial. However, the trust placed in personal relationships to manage these assets can be fraught with complications, leading to significant losses or legal and financial headaches.

Trusting Personal Relationships: The Risks and Realities

While you are away, your ability to oversee your property's maintenance, security, and legality is severely limited. Most of us want to turn to family members, close friends, or partners to handle our affairs, assuming those relationships are strong enough to protect these interests. However, this trust can expose assets to severe risks, as these individuals may lack the necessary experience or resources to manage a home, a vehicle, or other property.

Family members, for example, might have the best intentions but might need more experience or resources. A relative might be asked to cover property taxes, keep up with home maintenance, or ensure that a car stays insured and in good condition. Yet, if they don't have the financial means, know-how, or time, these tasks can fall by the wayside, leading to legal penalties, unexpected costs, or deteriorating property value you will deal with.

Trusting friends or partners can be even more precarious, mainly when the strain of incarceration will most likely test your relationship. Friendships or romantic relationships might weaken over time, leading to negligence or even intentional misuse of the incarcerated person's property. In some cases, trusted individuals have been known to sell cars without permission, allow homes to fall into foreclosure, or use bank accounts for personal gain.

Managing Homes and Property

Owning real estate while in prison presents one of the biggest challenges. A home requires constant upkeep—mortgage payments, property taxes, utilities, and general maintenance. If any of these responsibilities are neglected, the consequences can be severe. Missed mortgage payments can lead to foreclosure, and unpaid taxes can result in liens on the property or, worse, auctioning off the property over time.

Even if someone handles the finances, there's the physical side of things to consider. Houses need repairs, lawns need mowing, and empty homes are at risk of vandalism or squatting. I've seen cases where well-intentioned family members couldn't manage these tasks, and homes fell into disrepair, losing significant value by the time the owner was released.

Issues can still arise when a tenant manages the property on behalf of the incarcerated owner. Tenants may stop paying rent, or damage may go unnoticed without regular inspections. The legal process of evicting a non-paying or destructive tenant is complicated for anyone, let alone someone behind bars.

The Risks of Owning a Vehicle

Cars may seem more straightforward to manage, but they come with their own set of challenges. Vehicles need to be insured, registered, and properly maintained. Many people arrange for a family member or friend to "borrow" the car while they're serving time. While this can seem like a mutually beneficial arrangement, problems can quickly arise. If the borrower gets into an accident or incurs traffic violations, the incarcerated owner could be liable, depending on the insurance situation.

Too often, the person caring for the car might let it fall into disrepair. Simple things like oil changes or keeping the battery charged can be forgotten, resulting in costly repairs or even rendering the car undrivable when the owner is released. Worse, the vehicle may be used in ways the owner didn't anticipate—incurring traffic violations, being impounded, or even becoming involved in criminal activity. All of these problems and expenses become yours to deal with when you get out, and you've lost the value of the auto to use to buy another one. Sell it before you go in and put the money in the bank. This is the same for motorcycles and smaller items.

Financial Assets and Bank Accounts

Beyond physical assets like homes and vehicles, managing financial accounts presents another area where trust can be abused. Often, it seems to make sense to give a family member or partner Power of Attorney to access their finances while they're inside. This can help ensure that bills are paid and money is available for commissary or legal expenses. However, it also gives the person managing the account free rein to misuse funds.

Even with the best intentions, the person in charge of these accounts might have different priorities than you, and you cannot hold their feet to the fire. Bills may go unpaid, or personal expenses might drain the account. I've seen people come out of prison to find that their savings are gone, either through negligence or outright theft.

The Potential for Legal and Financial Consequences

Failure to manage your property and assets while in prison can lead to significant legal and financial consequences. Unpaid bills can damage your credit scores, making it challenging to rebuild your financial standing upon release. Foreclosure on a home or repossession of a vehicle can leave you without the basic necessities to reintegrate into society, making it more challenging to start over.

If taxes or debts go unpaid, there's also the potential for lawsuits or liens against your property. This can create lasting legal battles that extend well beyond the prison sentence, further delaying rehabilitation and financial stability.

The Importance of Proper Planning

Proper planning before prison is the best way to avoid these pitfalls. It's crucial to carefully select the individuals who will manage your assets and ensure they have the resources and skills to do so responsibly. Legal arrangements like durable powers of attorney or property management agreements can help create more precise boundaries and provide legal recourse if something goes wrong. But if it's your child or a spouse, you will most likely have the loss.

In many cases, selling assets before entering prison might be the most practical choice. Technology such as phones, personal computers, and tablets will all become dated and lose their value or disappear. You might consider having a garage sale, selling them now for the best price, and banking the cash. This could provide liquid funds to support commissary needs or legal fees and eliminate the stress of managing physical property from behind bars.

In summary, trusting others to care for your property while in Camp is a significant gamble. No matter how close, relationships can falter under time, distance, and financial responsibility pressures. Without proper safeguards, assets can deteriorate or disappear. All of this creates additional hardships for when you return and are already facing the immense challenge of rebuilding your life. If you own it, sell it.

Chapter Four

DROP AND ROLL

It's finally the day of self-surrender. You cannot take anyone inside, so say goodbye in the parking lot and enter the Camp facility alone. You will be greeted by an inmate or guard working there who will have a packet ready for you to complete. It is essential to review the details of this packet carefully. Is your name spelled correctly? Is the correct ID number provided in your initial letter also found in your pre-sentencing report? If you find any other personal details or items mis-spelled, print them correctly. This document spells out how many months you will be incarcerated, so it is vital to check and confirm that it is all correct. My packet showed all my personal information correctly but incorrectly had me jailed for 84 months, not 18. I refused to sign anything until they corrected the paperwork. They had placed someone else's time in my packet. This can happen, so you need to verify everything.

You won't be allowed ANY jewelry except a plain wedding band. Otherwise, these valuables will be held in a packet for you to collect when you leave. Even your shoes will be confiscated, so bring a pair you don't mind giving away. The facility will replace all your clothing with a standard white jumpsuit, a T-shirt, grandma panties, and a sports bra, so it is essential to know your sizes. They will give you a pair of slip-on canvas shoes you wear until you get suited out in the laundry facility.

Select an outfit you are willing to donate, including your shoes. You can have them keep this outfit, or they will send it back to your family. I did not want my family dealing with my things while I was away. This decision is a personal choice. All I could think of at that moment was when I would be strip-searched. That didn't happen. This action is up to the guard on duty if they want to do a body search.

You will also receive your PAC and PIN, which become your new identity during your stay. Your PAC is confidential and should not be shared with other inmates. A replacement fee will be charged if a PAC is misplaced or compromised. These numbers are the ones you use to log onto any equipment in the facility to communicate and show who you are. For example, when logging onto the computer, they will ask for each of these numbers to pull up any material that is related to you. It may take 24 to 48 hours to get your PAC and PIN from the FCI (the main prison on site), but these are necessary to access emails, phones, the commissary, or anything else you might need.

They will take your fingerprints and a photo to make your lanyard. Do not lose this. You can be stopped any-time and anywhere at the Camp and asked to see your lanyard. It is supposed to be worn around your neck at all times except when you sleep. You can get written up if you are found without it.

It's now time for a brief meeting with a Camp coun-selor. They will bring you to their office and ask you a few questions like: What did you do? How are you feeling? Do you or have you felt suicidal? Have you felt that way in the last several days? Are you or have you recently taken any drugs or alcohol? These questions are mainly asked to see if they need to put you in isolation initially and watch for your safety. I strongly suggest you be honest in this process. The only woman I knew who faked it was not happy; she had to stay in isolation and was there for over 24 hours. Just suck it up, get through the process, and try to blend in.

The paperwork is complete and you are suited in your white jumpsuit and canvas shoes. You are now provided a bedroll and lanyard prepared for you. The bedroll contains two sets of sheets, your mattress, one wool blanket and four rolls of toilet paper. This is your bedding during your imprisonment.

Next, you head to Medical, where they will provide a limited exam. They weigh you, give you a TB shot, take your temperature, and check your blood pressure. They also do a quick eye exam and an initial dental exam at some point. You will also be scheduled with the Camp doctor to review your records, ask questions, and discuss any medication you are taking and why. The doctor then determines what medicine you will be provided while at the facility. It is entirely up to the doctor. All of your meds are generic now.

NOTE: If you are 60 or older or are disabled, now is when you need to ask for a "BUNK PASS." This pass allows you a lower bunk bed. These passes are precious, but many have managed to get them, so if it's important for you to have one, get it now. Depending on your age and disability, the guard will determine who gets the lower bunk. With your bedroll and bright white jumpsuit, you now have the honor of doing the "walk of shame." You must remember that every woman in there who is now checking you out as a newcomer has had to do this.

If the facility has a Big Sister program on-site, someone should arrive during your initial medical visit and take you to get settled. You might get lucky and receive a welcome packet, but there are no guarantees. When you check-in, you get nothing but bedding and an initial outfit, so these gifts are valuable. You might get a toothbrush, comb, mini portions of shampoo, a writing pad, pencil, and snack food in this care packet. If the program is good, you may be able to access some casual clothing and a pair of tennis shoes.

Your Big Sister will also fill you in on the rules and give you a tour of the facility. They will provide you with the lay of the land about the place, the guards, and the people. It would be best if you remembered it's a perspective. One thing you hear quickly is "not to pet the puppies." While it seemed weird to me, I quickly realized that there could be some very needy or disturbed people here, and you need to get to know everyone cautiously. If someone gives you something, you must be careful when accepting it and ensure it doesn't come with any conditions you might not want to meet.

Your new living quarter is called the "bus stop." It's a 20 x 20 foot-room with five iron bunk beds. These are twin beds with flat metal bases or springs where several of them have sprung. If you get a top bunk, you will climb a thick metal ladder that is as uncomfortable to climb as it sounds. No rails exist, and you might not be against a wall. I always worried about rolling over and falling out. There are also 10 gray or tan-colored lockers. Eventually, you can buy a lock for it to protect all of your worldly possessions found inside. Of course, the most valuable things you have are all the legal and personal papers you brought with you. One of these beds and lockers will be your home for the next 90 days or so.

These bus stops sit at the entry of one of four different alleys where the women live. Eventually, you will be assigned a bed in one of these locations. The bus stops are for people who are in trouble and new people. Living in these rooms is like living in a fishbowl because you are so visible to all who pass by. They are centrally located with large pane windows across the front. The walls are cylinder blocks, and one of my bunkies told me they are just like the ones in her home in the projects where she lived when she was younger. Every surface here is hard, dirty, and uninviting. There is no privacy, but the bus stops may have views to the outside.

At each of these entries, a row of pay phones is available to all living in that alley of the building. Right beside the phones is a large entry to the showers. As you enter, it's a relief to see individual showers. Just beyond the wall of showers, you will find a long vanity full of several sinks and a large mirror that fills the wall above the vanity. While everything gets mopped daily and the 50-gallon trash cans emptied regularly – the place is just filthy. Mold holds many of the tiles on the shower walls and some of the tiles overhead. Of course, the tile could be missing entirely.

At the end of the vanity on both sides is a metal bin filled with what looks like discarded and used blow dryers, curling irons, and a flat iron, if you are lucky. All of these items are used in abundance by women as they dress for work or weekends and holidays. I consider myself fortunate because I like a cool room to sleep in. Having grown up in an extensive family, I am comforted by a lot of noise. For many occupants, the noise was the most challenging thing. You now live with approximately 75 women in each of the four sections that have become your new living quarters. Some women sat wearing blankets in their beds because they were so cold.

Once you have your PAC and PIN numbers provided by the main facility, which can take up to 48 hours, you can set up your email and phone on the computer. The Trust Fund Limited Inmate Computer System (TRULINCS) is the inmate network that provides inmates access to multiple services. At no time do the inmates have any access to the Internet. Every time you use the computer, you have a time limit per use. The email system CORRLINKS is not free, is monitored, and is limited to 100 persons on your list. When you first contact your person, they must accept the original link via email. Otherwise, you can't communicate. Plan on using the computer for about five cents a minute. When your time is up, it stops working, so you learn to keep track of the time. This automatic shut-off is good since so many women are trying to use so few monitors.

There is often a line. You need to allow extra time to enter your information into the system to use everything properly. You can get Call-Out information on the computer. These are also provided on a sheet in writing in the foyer every night after the mail call. This information tells you where you must be the following day if someone in administration or one of the guards has scheduled you.

In TRULINCS there is a tab where you can purchase songs to download to their version of an iPod (MP3 player). You can find these used but they may only last for a short time as they connect to those PAC/PIN I told you about, and they must be refreshed every 30 days to work. They are purchased through the commissary and are pricey. You can upgrade your earbuds since these get a lot of use. Earbuds are necessary to watch television in one of the two TV rooms or to watch movies shown in the gym on Friday nights. You can only access the TVs, movies, or music with earbuds.

The Inmate Telephone System is called TRUFONE. Each inmate will use their PAC & PIN to access TRUFONE, including instructions for use of this system. In addition, each inmate will need to perform voice verification registration. It's important to keep your voice calm and even when recording your name for the first time. You will have to say your name the same way **every time** you make a phone call. Management of inmates' telephone numbers is performed via the TRULINCS system. There also a time limit on each phone call as the phones are so busy. The maximum you can be on at one time is 15 minutes. A recording goes off every five minutes, letting the person on the other side of the phone know they are talking to a Federal Inmate. One of the ladies who did not want her grandson to know where she was, cleverly selected to have the recording in Spanish.

I would be remiss if I failed to discuss the public announcement (PA) system. This thing goes off before sunrise and continues until after 10 p.m. every day of the week. It is one of the more difficult things to get used to. It's like being in a hospital where someone is continuously being paged for something. You might hear your name being blasted over the campus at 5:30 in the morning if you got contraband in your mail. The CO uses the PA system to call their staff to work in the morning; occasionally, a guard might provide a soothing good morning and give a weather report. There are calls to come to class, to medical, to dental, to the administration offices, to the visiting room, and for a town driver to drive someone. You have to wait to be called to go for dinner every evening. You get called to pick up mail or to the chapel for personal news. This one is usually not good news as they are sharing that someone has been taken ill or has died.

Another one you won't care for is when they announce there is fog outside. You cannot go outside if the grounds are not visible to the guards. Now, there are no fences, gates, or guards outside to watch you, and if you try to run away, they add five years to your sentence. This addition, and your remaining time, won't be done at a Camp, so I failed to understand this. They announce a body count daily at 4 p.m. and 10 p.m. On weekends and holidays, they announce one at 10 am. From time to time, we all wondered if we were institutionalized, where we would automatically stand up to be counted after release.

Standing in a line is one way a great deal of time gets spent. There are lines to get your meals, to deliver or pick up laundry, to go to the commissary, and to get anything medical, including a "pill-call," which happens twice a day. There are lines to see your counselor or case manager and pick up your female hygiene products monthly. Twice a year, there are lines to get winter coats or spring jackets for the season. Trust me, you will spend a lot of time in many lines every day.

Chapter Five

COMMISSARY

Going to the commissary to shop can be overwhelming. First, before you arrive at Camp, you must determine what budget you can afford to allocate to your commissary purchases while confined. You can decide what is left once you've planned for your family responsibilities. With these funds, there are many things you can purchase and will need from the commissary.

Second, if you owe restitution, the prison will deduct $25.00 a month from any funds you have available. The Camp will allow you to carry a maximum of $500.00 on your books. However, the commissary will only allow you to spend up to $360.00 per month as of 2024. Let's say you are working at a job for $25 a month; they will take these funds before you can spend them. If you have paid restitution or don't owe any (including court fees), you must bring proof of this payment with your legal papers to show to your Camp counselor to ensure they don't take your funds. If you don't have proof, they take the $25.00 until you can show proof of payment.

While the women from Camp stock and inventory items, the guard rings up each purchase to ensure it is posted against your PAC and PIN. There is a commissary form to complete requesting the items you want to purchase. The form lets you total your spending in advance to try and help avoid overspending.

However, the guard will not let you spend funds you do not have. It's nice to know in advance what you believe you are paying. This form is a hard copy of your requests with your personal information that the guard keeps for his records. Remember to request a new form every time you shop for the following week. If you don't have a form, go to the front and tell the women in line you need to request one.

The commissary is open Tuesdays through Thursdays, and those who can shop are scheduled alphabetically to shop on a certain day. While it opens at 7 am each morning, the lines start well before it opens. The line gets long quickly, and it can take nearly an hour to get through on some days. It closes by noon if they are not very busy. Everyone comes early to buy items they want before they are sold out. Many must shop before work (some women work off-site and are gone all day). The guard will announce on the PA system that the commissary is open. They provide a fifteen-minute warning when they are about to close.

An essential piece of information is that you may ONLY shop on your scheduled day. They may announce they are closing for regular shopping and will now be available for special orders. If you've ordered something like tennis shoes, a craft item, bras, etc., they will call your name when that order arrives for you to pick up. Try on or carefully inspect whatever your order is then and there. Once you leave the counter, the item is yours and cannot be returned or refunded. If it is a specialty kit with beads, yarn, or a kit, inspect it for being complete when you pick it up, or you will not be able to return it if there is a problem. I am providing a web link in the back of the book to an order sheet to review and better understand what you may purchase in the commissary. For available specialty items, you need to find out who turns in specialty orders for crafts because the commissary does not always handle these orders.

Even if you have sufficient funds, you are limited by the Camp's budget of what you can spend weekly. When figuring out what you can spend, you first need to allocate some of your funds into accessing the computer and time on the phone. The phones cost roughly fifteen cents per minute, and email access is approximately five cents a minute. You are not using these funds when just reading things on the computer in your file (like the Call-Out sheet showing appointments). It doesn't take email time to shop for music for your MP3 player, but each tune costs $1.25. The MP3 player has to be validated every 30 days to stay operational, or it stops working on the last day you scheduled. (This is one reason you don't want to buy a used one, as they will not work for long). After determining your budget for emails and phones, you can see what you have left over to shop.

Some of the first things on your shopping list will be soap, shampoo, a brush, toothbrush, toothpaste, lotion, and any essential toiletries you need. None of these come with your original bed package. You will get four rolls of toilet paper; if you need more, put it on the list. Toilet paper is now your entire paper inventory. Think napkins, paper towels, Kleenex, make-up wipes, and toilet paper.

In 2017, the BOP determined they should provide a monthly allotment of feminine hygiene products. Once a month, when turning in sheets for clean ones, you may collect a variety of these items totaling no more than 40. For several women with health issues, this is not adequate. If the supply is insufficient, add these to your items needed when shopping.

Buying the initial things you need can take up to six weeks before you can shop for extras from your allotted budget. Most items come from Walmart, and there is a thirty percent markup on every item for a prisoner's fund. Things are expensive, as you will see when reviewing the list in the back. An MP3 player with basic earbuds costs between $25 to $50.00. You will need this if you want to listen to anything while there.

You will need a pair of sweatpants, a couple of T-shirts, sweatshirts, and socks to replace the large men's socks provided. Remember that everything you buy comes in men's sizes, so before you arrive, find out what your sizes are—that goes for tennis shoes and boots. Extra socks, sports bras, and limited casual clothing are some of the first things you might buy. Laundry is once a week, so you need enough of everything to make it through the wash cycle. If you work out, you might need more casual clothes and socks.

They will provide you with seven pairs of granny panties, seven sports bras, and your dress greens (or whatever color your Camp uses) that you must wear during working hours, anytime you come to the administrative offices or the visiting room. These dress greens were provided the first weekday after you arrive when you are taken to the laundry to get your items. You are provided two pairs of pants, three dress shirts (that must be worn tucked in), five t-shirts, men's socks, sports bras, granny panties, a belt, steel-toed boots, and a seasonal coat or jacket. These are all men's sizes, so know what size you wear before arriving. You will turn in your canvas shoes and your white jumpsuit.

After a couple of months, you can buy some of the extras. You might want to buy clear plastic bags to hold your toiletries or food items: cups of noodles, tuna pouches, condiments, and limited make-up from cleansing to regular make-up. Around the holidays, they have special inventory items you can buy, such as perfume, make-up kits, and special junk food treats. All of the food at the commissary is junk food for the most part. There are casual clothes, socks, women's hygiene products, vitamins, etc. You can also purchase plastic bowls, utensils, large coffee cups, and large water glasses with lids, hair color, chips, postage stamps, birthday cards, and candy.

One more item for discussion is that you can buy many services and products that are not sold through the commissary. These are items or services that the other inmates make or provide for a set amount. The only way to pay for these things is to buy items they want from the commissary in an amount equal to their service or item provided to you. You want to buy and handle these payments before you purchase things for yourself. You must stay current on your bills with these women. It is not good to be identified as someone who doesn't pay their bills.

Chapter Six

SHOTS FIRED—ADDING TIME

While you are incarcerated, the BOP will keep you updated with your immunization shots. However, there is another type of "shot" you will want to avoid. A shot while incarcerated is when an inmate gets written up for breaking the rules or bad behavior, which can be very subjective. With each of these, the warden will determine the amount of good time you might lose. They can add more time to your sentence if you've lost all good time available. These are to be taken very seriously. I have a list of behaviors that will get you a shot later in this chapter.

When you are sentenced to a federal facility, you can earn a fifteen percent reduction in the time you will serve based on good behavior. This reduction means following the rules of the location where you are. That can seem daunting. Other institutions, like state and local prisons, can let you out for time served because they are too full and need the space. There is often no rhyme or reason for time served. It's also important to note that while you start with fifteen percent off, you may lose good time by getting a shot (or getting in trouble). It's also possible to get in trouble often enough that time gets added to your sentence, so it is crucial to understand the rules.

The time you serve is figured in months, so your initial sentence might be 18 months or 12 months and a day. By just adding that day, they reduce your time to eight months. Any sentence over twelve months automatically allows for a fifteen percent credit for good time. If you get twelve months or less, you are ineligible for good time off. But since we are talking about shots and not time served, please remember that you can get more time added by getting shots. It's helpful to take in a calendar and start marking your time off based on your good behavior time instead of the time you're sentenced.

It's also important to realize that while there are many rules, they can be imposed or tweaked based on the mood of the guard on duty. If they are in a bad mood, you need to steer clear and avoid any interactions if possible. The biggest problem I found with rules in Camp is that they are subject to the interpretation of the person giving the shot for breaking the rules. You can appeal it, but they lean toward the decision of the person who wrote the shot.

One rule is that you cannot discuss or do business in prison. This rule gets even more confusing when we discuss Prison Entrepreneurism. While I was in, I had to renegotiate my home loan, which was quite substantial. They thought I was working on a business loan because of the amount, and next thing you know, I'm being called on the PA system to come to the admin offices. From there, I was directed to the main FCI, where another guard gave me a written statement about what my shot was. I was horrified; the matter I was discussing was not work-related. It took writing an appeal and meeting with the Assistant Warden to get the shot removed. My point is that they are not easily removed once given out.

As I've said, every email, phone call, mail, or package is listened to or searched. You have to remember that at all times. Anything you say can be misinterpreted, so at least be aware that talking randomly, with no explanation to support your conversation, can lead to further questioning or problems. On another occasion, I walked into our dorm, and a huge fight had broken out just outside of it. I was stressed by the situation. I phoned my husband that afternoon and told him about it; next thing you know, I was pulled into the admin offices to see what I learned about the situation or if I was involved. I was so new I didn't even know the women. My point is that it is easy to get caught in the crossfire by discussing something you are not a part of.

Other things that may get you a shot:

- Failing to show up or stand up for counts
- Failing to make your bed by 7 am each morning
- Failing to show up for required GED classes when you are scheduled
- It should not have to be said, but smoking
- Any use of alcohol or the items found in your possession that could be turned into alcohol
- Food brought from the cafeteria unless it is a sack lunch dinner provided by them
- Anything in your possession that you do not have the original receipts for to prove you purchased them

- Going outside after they have had last call for going inside
- Fighting
- Letting any other inmate share the phone or video chat with you while in use
- Wearing casual clothes to the admin offices for any reason
- Not having your dress shirt tucked in when moving about the campus
- Failure to wear your dress greens anywhere but to the gym and in your dorm during business hours
- Being disrespectful to the guard, Camp manager, or counselor
- Getting excessive mail that is not within the guidelines provided (this means no glitter, no stamps, no empty pieces of paper or index cards, hardcover books that do not come directly from Amazon, and more; this is one I found was subject to the mood of the guard)
- No cooking in the dorms
- Having extra clothes or bedding beyond that allocated
- Having a pillow
- Excessive books in your room (I use room very loosely)
- Touching your visitor too often in the visiting room
- Talking to other people visiting other inmates in the visiting room
- Failure to wear your lanyard at all times when moving about the campus

- Going outside the dorm during a fog alert
- Leaving your dorm during a lockdown (since we are part of a men's prison system, we could find ourselves under lockdown because the men's prison went into lockdown, and they needed more guards at their prison, so we had to stay in lockdown as well)
- Failing to show up for med calls, pill lines, insulin shot lines, or doctor appointments
- Sharing items with an inmate
- The possession of jewelry, make-up, nail polish, bleach or hair products not sold from the commissary and you have a receipt to prove the purchase
- Not showing up for your job as scheduled
- Purchasing anything from another inmate

You can get a shot for countless things, and so many of them are part of your daily routine that it gets confusing. You will figure it out, but as mentioned earlier, you need to know that you can get shots for any of the above.

It is important to remember that the walls have eyes and ears, and anything can be easily misunderstood or misinterpreted when overheard. Plenty of Camp snitches have also befriended a guard or two who might have their own agenda. Remember that you are not making life friends or trying to impress anyone, so keep your personal life personal. You will make friends and find people to dine and hang out with; pick your friends wisely.

Shots can be incurred during a shakedown. These can be extreme or relatively focused. If one of the alleys

in a dorm has been a problem, the Camp can schedule one of these where the guards storm the alley like
a raid, surprising everyone, and they go through every
part of the alley they see fit to search. They throw mattresses, empty lockers, dump out laundry bags, and go
through everything, including patting down the women
in the dorm, checking pockets, etc. It is very unsettling.
Things get lost and broken. It takes a long time to get
organized and have the necessary things to be productive and live an everyday life. One of these can be very
unsettling weeks after it has occurred.

Another shakedown may be more focused; for
instance, the guard notices unusual jewelry or make-up,
or someone turns the woman into the guard. A few
guards may come to your bed and go through your
things. OR, they might call you to admin to give you
a shot, but they will wait until the guards go through
your locker to see if there is anything to add. On occasion, the woman will be taken to county (the local jail)
for breaking the rules so severely that they will pull all
of her items, put them in a laundry cart, and hold them
in admin until she returns, if she returns. This action
may result in being transferred to a more secure facility.
There are no guarantees your belongings will make it
through, and if they find illegal items, they will throw
them out. When you return from county, you return to
the bus stop and wait for your turn to be reassigned back
to a dorm, as you are now considered a troublemaker.

I am told that the guards on duty at the Camp are
supposed to select a few lockers each evening and go
through them. We often had one female guard for the

entire Camp, and there was no way she would have time to go through this process and keep up with the goings-on. When the guard is a man after hours, they will not even come to the dorms because they don't want to have any problems with the women. It has been known to have one of the women turn in a guard or admin staff for suggestive language or whatever, and then that person is taken off-site for some time until the situation is investigated. When I arrived, my dorm counselor was removed for almost six months while under investigation. This person's job is to approve your visitor's list or provide other administrative services and information while you are there. This role is frozen until the person is cleared or eventually replaced; it's unbelievable!

Chapter Seven
UNSAFE SANCTUARY

Some of the best advice I received before arriving at the Camp was to enjoy the bus stop. Its novelty, humor, and lifestyle are like nothing you will ever experience again. It is a temporary location, and some may even miss this experience. It is easier to learn the rules and count times in a group. I arrived on a holiday weekend. There are 10 a.m. counts on weekends and holidays. A count is a big deal in prison.

There are women at Camp who may be coming from a more restrictive FCI and have earned a less restrictive confinement. Everyone in the Camp is not necessarily a low-risk prisoner. I met women who killed their spouses, made and sold drugs, made counterfeit money, took social security checks, embezzled from someone, and more. It is every type of humanity; many have been there longer than you can imagine.

Everybody is ready to leave the bus stop and get into an alley. The dorm rooms hold three women (even though they were designed to hold two), and the alley holds about 48 women. The alley walls are about five feet tall, and your voice can be heard throughout the alley. Please remember at all times that the walls have ears. Yes, anything that you say or do, or someone in the alley thinks you say or do, can and will be used against you. Your opinion or side of the story to a guard, counselor, or case manager is only as reasonable as how much they know about you or how well they like the other inmate. If you are new, just shut up. You have no opinion and are sorry. You cannot win and need to remain low-key.

Every living quarter in the dorm has three lockers, three coat racks with four hooks, and one small desk with a stool in each to be shared. Lockers are an essential part of your camp life. One side of the locker has a couple of shelves that come in handy when organizing everything so you can find what you want or need. The other half needs shelves. Everyone is amazingly creative about how they build shelves and what they use. Girls would take a ceiling tile, cover it, and then place them on four screws. Others used FedEx boxes or pieces of other boxes for the same purpose.

You can hang your laundry bag (a long mesh bag with chords) on a peg. You hang your coat or jacket here as well. We would buy plastic totes. These would hold makeup in one, your spices and eating utensils in another, and your shower products in another. You should keep a folder containing your legal documents, commissary receipts, and completion certificates in your locker. Still, others might have vitamins and your meds if allowed to keep in your room.

Contraband is easily found in anyone's room. Contraband is anything in your possession that you did not buy directly from the commissary. There must be a receipt for proof of purchase—anything used outside its original intended purpose, i.e., cardboard boxes, tiles, and much more. If you buy and make something, you are supposed to send it home immediately. When you see others walking around with second-hand clothes or shoes, even if given to them, they are contraband—any earrings, bracelets, or nail polish. If you alter any greens (your daily suit-up clothes) or t-shirts (part of your uniform), it is considered the destruction of government property.

There is a chapel where you may go watch Christian movies most nights by scheduling them if there are no other group activities scheduled. Every Sunday most religions are represented and services are available. There is a library where inmates can check out books. There are limited classrooms where GED classes are taught to prepare the girls to enable them to pass their GED. There is a tiny media room where you can schedule to watch movies on a small computer if the room is available. In the administrative offices, a larger visiting room is used for various things when it's not time for visitors. The visiting room has a fenced-in patio and outdoor space for the kids to play or just get fresh air on a pretty day.

There is a large gym where a multitude of activities take place. The girls are most often found there in the evenings, if not in their rooms. Outside and just beyond the gym was a fairly large track. The track gets a lot of use. Sometimes, they have sports to participate in, but I didn't see many organized activities when I was there. Sitting quietly and listening to others talk will give you a better feel for the Camp. Without realizing it, this group can show you which guards are strict, rude, or mean. In my experience, if you are respectful to the guards and mind your own business, they are all okay for the most part.

Drama and gossip are off the charts. I was told early on, and I caution you to remember, "You can be anything you want to be in prison," including being "gay for the stay." Girls hold themselves out as wealthy, knowing high-powered people, pretending to be or knowing murderers, porn stars, or whatever they want to be. It isn't easy to understand what is and is not the truth.

Danger is always present. It is not unheard of to hear about someone being raped on campus. It's important to travel in pairs or groups. Don't assume because you are in prison that nothing bad can happen to you; like everything, you must know your surroundings and who you hang around.

Have you heard the term "lock in a sock?" This is where a girl puts a padlock in a sock and uses it as a weapon to go after someone. Again, fights can break out; people who have been there awhile don't care for new people. So be respectful and realize you are entering somewhere that is someone's home, and they may have been there a long time. Sudden or big changes do not sit well.

One scenario would be someone being sent to the SHU. This is 24-hour isolation with one hour outside each day. At my camp, we did not have the space for a SHU, so if you got into trouble you were sent to county. This experience can also cost you good time, add time to your existing sentence, or a shot on your record. Any or all of these can occur when you get in trouble.

The place can get very full when the Camp moves toward the time of year when they do budgets for the following year. They bring in a lot more ladies to get the numbers up, and the lines, the times, and everything else you do becomes extended and more complex. They can get so busy that they take away the TV rooms and use them for bus stops. It feels chaotic and unsettling during this time frame.

I am talking a lot about the women at Camp instead of the Camp itself. The real, meaningful experience and more difficult experiences come from your interactions with the girls, not the physical structure. As for the Camp, from the outside, it looks pretty and well-manicured. But there aren't enough benches for twenty-five percent of the women to sit outside. The guards come through and tell you to get off your beds and go out. Go where?

Inside the dorm, there still needs to be more seating available. There are two TV rooms with roughly thirty chairs. In a dorm of over 250 women, about half can watch TV. There are three TVs in each TV room. The available channels are scheduled; you need earbuds and an MP3 player to tune in and watch them. Those who can't or don't want to fit into the TV room can still watch movies in the gym on Friday nights. The Friday night movie is whatever the FCI men's prison selected to watch.

One of the scariest things about living anywhere in the Camp is if you get in trouble or have a medical problem. Remember that you can only call out with your limited minutes. Your family will not be able to call you. Once you have found a trusted friend, I suggest you exchange immediate family personal information. This is also why you need to have a Medical Power of Attorney form on file with the facility and your family so they know your intentions. Women do get very sick and even die in Camp. As a prison town driver, most of my trips took one or more ladies for medical treatments somewhere off campus. Your friend can contact your family and let them know you have been taken away for several reasons: relocated to another facility, taken somewhere to be deposed or be a witness for an open case, or taken to a hospital. The prison will not tell your family, and you are not in a position to contact them.

There are Camp snitches. They run to the guards with everything they see or hear. They use a "cop-out" form to complain. This is a form you can complete on the computer complaining to the administration about anything. These women complain if the menu changes from the schedule. Just as many women will complain if they don't change the menu. You can be turned in for talking, sleeping, snoring, fighting, being stuck up, not talking enough, being too nosey, or looking nosey. I think you get the picture.

Some girls do have the knowledge on what the rules say or what they do not. It can be confusing if you are at a Camp that doesn't follow these rules. But once here, you can see where basic rules provide stability and a calmer environment.

Chapter Eight
GET A JOB

One of the first things you'll need to figure out when you arrive at Camp is what you'll do during your sentence. Everyone will tell you to get a job—and they're right. You need one to make some income, and a job also helps you survive the long days. However, don't expect a big paycheck. Most jobs start at about $25 a month, and earning over $100 is rare. The real value in working comes from passing the time and staying busy.

Before you can get a job, you have to go through orientation. Orientation is a requirement, and until you complete it, you won't be eligible for any jobs. The issue is that orientations aren't always scheduled regularly. For example, when I arrived, the last one had just taken place, and it took months before they scheduled the next one.

Once you complete orientation, the next challenge is finding out which jobs are available. Many of the best jobs aren't openly posted; they're filled by word of mouth and recommendations. You'll need to pay attention, ask around, and befriend someone who can help get your foot in the door. The guards rely heavily on recommendations from other prisoners when filling jobs, especially for more desirable roles.

Here's a breakdown of the jobs commonly available. Each Camp has its own needs, but most of these jobs exist in some form across facilities.

Administrative Clerk

Administrative clerks work in various Camp offices. One typical example is the clerk who meets you when you first arrive. They prepare paperwork, organize bed-rolls, and turn you over to a counselor or guard for intake. Other clerical tasks include:

- Sorting and processing mail
- Preparing packages for outgoing shipments
- Organizing documents for guards and counselors

Clerical positions can also include:

- Working in the medical department
- Helping staff with paperwork
- Assisting in the visitor's room on visiting days

These jobs are in high demand and difficult to get since you'll work closely with guards and staff.

Town Driver

One of the most sought-after jobs, town driver, requires a recommendation and an interview with a guard and counselor to determine your trustworthiness. Surprisingly, it can be difficult to find women with valid driver's licenses, as many have been incarcerated so long that their licenses have expired. Town drivers transport inmates for medical or dental appointments, pick up and drop off new arrivals, and drive staff between the main facility (FCI) and the Camp. You might also take inmates to get their paperwork when they are released. The job is busy and comes with a lot of responsibility. It often involves working long hours—sometimes as early as 4 a.m. and until the last count at 10 p.m. It's also highly desirable because it allows you to leave the Camp regularly.

Instructors

Instructors work in the Camp's education department, helping inmates who do not have a GED to prepare for the test. Classes run Monday through Friday, with both morning and afternoon sessions. As an instructor, you might teach multiple classes or focus on one area of the GED curriculum. Camps also offer night classes, and if you have a skill or expertise, you can propose a class to the education manager. If approved, the Camp will put out a sign-up sheet, and if at least ten women enroll, you'll get to teach. This job requires references and word of mouth, as it involves close interaction with staff.

Librarian

The librarian position also falls under the education department. You'll manage the Camp's book inventory, check in new books, remove outdated ones, and transfer materials between the Camp and the main FCI.

You'll also be responsible for checking dorms for unreturned books and organizing the library. Occasionally, other inmates might volunteer to help, but this is largely a solo job that requires a good deal of organization.

Cafeteria Jobs

The head cook is the most powerful position in the cafeteria, often held by someone with previous cooking experience. This job involves menu planning, food ordering, and overseeing the kitchen staff. The head cook also helps prepare hundreds of sack lunches for the FCI during lockdowns, feeding over 1,000 inmates daily. Beyond the head cook, there are positions in food prep, serving on the line, dishwashing, and clean-up. While the top jobs are highly competitive, other cafeteria roles are usually available, and they offer consistent work with a predictable routine.

Environmental Jobs

These jobs involve sorting, recycling, and handling the Camp's trash. The work is tough and often dirty, but it pays a little better than some less demanding jobs. The hours are long and not a popular choice, but it's a stable position for someone willing to put in the effort.

Laundry

These are essential roles, and the laundry team is where you'll first be issued your prison greens upon arrival.

They are skilled in sizing and will ensure you have the right fit. Each day, they collect laundry from all sections of the facility and process it through commercial washers and dryers, managing both the flow and schedule with efficiency. If you need to exchange clothes, request a winter coat, or search for any donated items, laundry is your go-to. The team is also responsible for identifying unmarked or lost bags of clothing. Occasionally, inmates forget to secure their bags properly, causing clothes to spill and mix with others. This happens more often than you'd think, and it can be quite frustrating when it's your belongings affected. With 250 to 300 women to account for, sorting out misplaced clothing can be challenging.

Chapel Administrator

As the chapel administrator, you'll support the various religious services offered at the Camp. This job involves managing inventory for religious supplies, setting up rooms for services, and handling orders for the chaplain. One of the perks is access to a private office and a TV, which you can use any time before 9 p.m. It's a relatively low-stress job, but it requires attention to detail and a basic understanding of the needs of different religious groups.

Gym Administrator

The gym administrator oversees all the activities in the Camp's gym, including workout classes, events, and maintaining equipment. You'll also manage special events like GED graduations or movie nights. The job is busy, as the gym is often occupied by inmates working out, playing cards, or doing puzzles. Like the chapel administrator, this job comes with office and TV privileges but requires coordinating with the recreation guard, who oversees both the men's and women's facilities.

Specialty Jobs (HVAC, Welding, etc.)

You can work in these departments if you have experience in skilled trades like HVAC or welding. These jobs involve practical work, like repairs and maintenance, and are supervised by guards with expertise in these areas. It's an excellent way to use your skills and stay busy with hands-on tasks.

Warehouse

Warehouse jobs involve receiving shipments, checking inventory, and distributing supplies between the Camp and the main FCI. They're physically demanding, as most of the work is done on the docks, and there is a lot of exposure to the outdoors. However, they're a good option for someone who doesn't mind manual labor.

Safety Officer

Safety officers are responsible for conducting checks around the Camp to ensure everything is in working order.

This work includes testing batteries, inspecting equipment, and reporting any issues that need repairs. It's a maintenance-focused role that requires attention to detail and consistency.

Motor Pool

The motor pool maintains the Camp's vehicles, which include vans, buses, and cars. This job involves routine vehicle maintenance, including oil changes, tire repairs, and tune-ups. If you're certified to drive, you might also be assigned a vehicle to use for transporting staff or inmates.

Maintenance

The maintenance staff is responsible for keeping the Camp clean and functional. This work includes emptying trash cans, mopping, and cleaning shared spaces like bathrooms and hallways. Many women are needed to keep up with the Camp's cleaning needs, and one of the jobs involves supervising others to ensure everything gets done.

In addition to these standard jobs, many Camps offer unique positions. For example, my Camp had a *Big Sisters* program, where someone was in charge of distributing supplies like toothbrushes and pads of paper to new arrivals. We also had a *dog program* where inmates could train dogs for service work or help at local shelters. These opportunities depend on the relationships between the Camp and the surrounding community.

Jobs in Camp might not pay much, and they won't lead to career advancement, but they help you pass the time and stay productive. Figuring out what role suits you best—and making the right connections—can make your time a little more manageable.

Chapter Nine
THE PRISON ENTREPRENEUR

Spending time in prison was a constant contradiction of expectations and rules. The rules tell you clearly that you cannot have anything in your possession that you did not buy directly from the commissary or was not issued to you by the BOP. And then, upon arrival, you find an abundance of services and products to purchase from the other inmates. The business owner in me found this exciting and scary at the same time. Most ladies here believed they weren't smart enough to accomplish much. Yet, here they were, using their God-given talents to generate commissary credits to support themselves—all as thriving entrepreneurs. These women would have had little to no income to survive without these side gigs. Here is an example of some of the many things available.

One enterprise was operating a laundry pool, which entailed collecting someone's laundry bag and getting in line to turn it in on laundry days. The inmate would designate it for washing only. When the laundry department returned the bags to the dorm, they would be collected by this pool by the inmate's name. The damp clothes were taken to the dorm laundry room to dry and fold. It was very helpful if you had a job or could afford to do this. Typical laundry at Camp was washing and drying all the bags in huge loads and returning them all clumped up and wrinkled as they often sat for a bit before the woman could get to them to unpack. You could also request all or some of the items be ironed. It was a reasonable service, but you had to have the budget for it. Several groups of women did this as a side hustle.

You could pay someone to create more shelves in your locker and organize it so that you can store more and find things quickly. Some people have a fantastic talent for using the resources available and knowing how to store things.

Others would charge to alter men's clothing so the outfit had some form or fit. Sometimes, you just needed a hem or your socks shortened. Often, you could get second-hand clothes, but they might require a little more altering. Remember, this could be considered the destruction of government property.

To give you a general idea, you could get pedicures, manicures, massages, hair braiding, eyebrow threading, and your hair cut and colored. You could also get a makeover, get your makeup done for a photo day, or visitors. The women were resourceful, creative, and very talented. These were some of the many services available. Services were easier to get away with because someone did something for you, and there was no apparent exchange of goods.

All of these services had a set price, and when you ordered the service, the woman providing it would give you a list of items she wanted from the commissary. The Camp's primary payment source is paying someone with goods purchased from the commissary. The only other payment method is if you have a service or item on hand to barter. I will say it often: all of these things are illegal and against the rules, so if you get caught, you are subject to a shot.

The list of things to buy is staggering. You could buy pillows, pillowcases, used clothing, makeup, nail polish, and jewelry, from earrings to hair berets. Where the variety of colors of nail polish, blush, or eye-shadow came from was a mystery as most of it was not sold at commissary.

Then there are the ladies' talents to produce crafts and art for sale. Again, the rule says that once you've made something, you must immediately send it home and off campus. These women do remarkable etchings and can paint designs on almost any object you own. Extraordinary items can be found with intricate beading. Rosaries, bracelets, and rings are all for the asking.

The most adorable yarn animals made by these ladies could quickly be sold for profit to the public. I wish there were a way to help these women set up a site to sell their products. However, conducting business is strictly prohibited. You will lose good time being involved in these actions. I was constantly amazed by the love and care that went into these products. Some women knitted beanies and berets, while others beaded or painted initials on items.

If you think this is not running a business, you must realize that these women are identifying a need. They are resourcing their products and marketing them to their customers. They organize and procure bulk items and maintain them to fill the orders. There are often many customers, and each may ask for different things that must be tracked – everything from size, colors, quantity, and deadlines.

Then, there is dealing with payment for goods and services. The entrepreneur has to submit her bill, keep track of who owes her what, and make sure she collects from everyone each week. It takes a while to get used to what you can spend for yourself at the commissary, so I cannot imagine keeping track of and getting paid for all of these different products and services without technology. It's overwhelming, but they seem to do it without a hitch. It can be complicated, but one woman in the Camp had everything made, including decorations, party favors, and gifts for a group of eight to be sent home for her son's third birthday. Just the postage would be out of this world.

There was always plenty to choose from when sending home gifts for birthdays and Christmas, which was a relief because it was one of the things I worried about. The birthday and Christmas cards were like nothing you've seen. I sent a 3-D birthday card to my husband for the birthday I was missing. It made me feel like I was participating. This woman had a permanent table in the gym where she worked, created, took orders, and delivered constantly.

Now, let's discuss the private food industry within the Camp. Women could "borrow" items from the cafeteria, buy them off the commissary, or purchase them through the warehouse's back door. With these goods, they would take orders in advance for Friday nights to buy all kinds of desserts and treats. You had to find the woman and get your name in before she prepared the ill-gotten goodies. On the weekends, the women purchased most of the extra food, dressed in their altered clothing, were made up to the nines, and had treats available for Friday movie nights. I bought an enchilada that was made from scratch, which was amazing. I snuck one of them into my husband to try on visitors' a day, and he wanted to know if I had more.

You could live a decent life if your budget allowed. For those of you who are thinking, "Hey, these guys are in prison, they are supposed to suffer." Let me tell you that there is no way to describe how painful and ongoing it is to be removed from everything you know and have contact, if you're lucky, ten minutes a day by phone. Yes, you are improving your life as much as possible, but spending holidays, let alone all the rest of your time with strangers, is daunting, lonely, and painful. A Merry Christmas or Happy Birthday call with a smile comes through a held back blizzard of tears.

While inmates aren't supposed to buy or possess any of these things, there would be open flea markets selling items many weekends. There might be a garage sale for one of the alleys on another weekend. This occurred more often when a large group relocated to another Camp. Transferees would be limited in what they could take if transferred, definitely not the illegal things they possessed—so there would be a fire sale.

I'm closing this chapter with a reminder that during a shakedown, individually or as a group, you could get a shot and lose good time if you are transferred or just found with items purchased without a commissary receipt. I also wish these women would remember these fantastic skills and abilities when they leave. I hope they use the resources, creativity, and skills they have demonstrated to make a living when they get out. I wish the Camp could do more to recognize and reinforce these skills so the women could gain the confidence they need to live better. Now, that might be a form of rehabilitation.

Chapter Ten

UNDER THE MICROSCOPE

Every prison handles its visiting room differently, and often, the experience is shaped by the mood of the guards on duty. Rules that seem set in stone can suddenly be enforced more strictly or relaxed, depending on the day. Remember that when you fill out your Pre-Sentencing Report before sentencing, you must list your immediate relatives. If they aren't listed, they'll need to complete a form for approval, which can take some time. Only once approved will they be allowed to visit. You are allowed a maximum of 10 visitors on your list at any given time.

In my case, the Camp I was sent to was located beside a much larger facility. The Camp looked more like administrative offices, and visitors could easily miss the entrance and end up at the main prison instead. My oldest son made this mistake during his first visit. He unknowingly entered the high-security facility, navigating barbed wire and screenings, before realizing he was in the wrong place. They redirected him to the Camp when he mentioned he was there to see his mother. The experience horrified him, and I felt terrible.

The visiting room at the Camp had its own unique set of rules. Unfortunately, your visitors will feel like they are being treated like prisoners themselves. This is off-putting and can cause more concern about how you are treated inside. The guards expect you to know the rules, even though they can make them more challenging or random. While all the literature tells the reader that they promote visits and family time, this is just a job for them, and many provide no empathy or help in getting through the process. I watched my youngest son calm himself after I got there, and he cleared the guards. He hated vising because he always felt like he was being treated like a criminal.

Coming to visit someone in prison, even a Camp, is a stressful and intimidating experience for anyone not used to dealing with this environment. Visitors can't wear specific colors, especially those that match our uniforms. Though these colors can be chosen at random by the guard, Open-toed shoes were also prohibited. Visitors had to empty their pockets and could only bring their car keys and a driver's license. No bags, purses, or containers were allowed, which made things tricky for visitors with babies. Women's clothing was scrutinized more than men's, and if a guard was in a nasty mood, they might send a guest to a local store to buy something more appropriate to wear before admitting them.

For many visitors, the experience was nerve-wracking enough without feeling like they, too, were being treated like prisoners. The guards weren't always helpful, and if guests didn't check in by 9 a.m., they could end up waiting in their car for hours until the daily count was completed. This wait meant the inmate would be sitting on the other side, fully dressed, waiting for a visit that was delayed, losing precious time together.

Visitors also needed cash to buy anything, which meant purchasing a $5 card outside the visiting room to use at the vending machines, which don't accept cash. You could load the $5 card up to the value of $100 for use on any of the vending machines inside the visiting room. For families traveling with children, it could be a long, tiring day if they didn't have food or drinks.

Once inside, guests would wait for us to arrive. We had to be dressed in our prison greens and check in with the guard, handing over our lanyards while we were in the visiting room. At this Camp, we could briefly hug our loved ones upon arrival, but physical contact was limited. The seating arrangements varied depending on the guard—sometimes we sat across from each other, other times side by side. There were separate bathroom facilities for visitors.

The Camp had a small game room with well-worn board games. When I asked if I could donate new games, I was told this was only allowed if donated through specific charities. Still, despite the worn condition, families often played together, and there was even an outdoor area with benches where we could sit, though a fenced-in concrete pad surrounded it. The irony was that this was the only fenced area in the Camp.

A guard check of inmates took place mid-morning. All inmates lined up while the guards called our names, requiring us to state our ID numbers. We would then walk to the other side of the room before resuming our visits. I always found this process unnecessarily dehumanizing, particularly for those with children present.

Then there were the guards who came from higher-security prisons or were just plain rude. They would pace the room, looking for infractions. Even friendly exchanges between different visitors could draw attention, with the guard interrupting to ask, "Who is your visitor?" and reminding us to talk only to our designated guest.

When it was time for the visit to end, we had to wait for the guard to let us back into the Camp. Sometimes, this meant a body search. A new guard frequently targeted one of my bunkmates, and seemed to have it out for her. The guard would make her husband buy a new shirt despite it being the same one he'd worn the day before. When my bunkmate returned to the Camp, she was always strip-searched. At one point, the guard forced her to squat and wait, using it as a power play. Eventually, many women stopped having visitors because they didn't want to endure the humiliation of a strip search after each visit. These searches were not typical unless you were suspected of breaking rules, but some guards bent the rules based on their own biases.

The visiting room was a deeply emotional place. It was where families reunited, sometimes after years apart. I'll never forget one woman who hadn't had a visitor in seven years. When her sister finally came to see her, they ran to each other, embracing and crying, which brought the entire room to tears.

Despite the challenges, I encourage staying connected with loved ones during your time. Maintaining those bonds can make a significant difference when it comes time to re-enter the world. The visiting room might be full of restrictions, but it's also full of hope and reconnection.

Chapter Eleven

FAITH BEHIND BARS

In the sterile, cold confines of a women's prison camp, faith often becomes both refuge and battleground. For many women in the Camp, religion offers a sense of identity, a form of community, and, at times, the only consistent structure in lives otherwise stripped of control. But faith in prison is not just about belief; it is entangled with survival, power, and the search for redemption.

Religion behind bars is as much about the rituals of comfort as the desperate search for meaning. Women come from all walks of life, and while some arrive with faith already ingrained, others discover it in the bleakness of their surroundings. Christian services may dominate in many facilities, but prisons are microcosms of society, serving diverse religious practices: Islam, Judaism, Hinduism, Wiccan, Buddhism, Native American, and newer spiritual movements. This diversity of faiths is a testament to the resilience and adaptability of the human spirit. Some women come to faith organically, drawn by the solace of prayer or the need for forgiveness. Others are influenced by the simple, undeniable fact that religious groups tend to offer resources that no other faction inside the prison can provide: spiritual counseling and frequency of routine.

Our chapel was a large room set aside for various services. Here, we all sat shoulder to shoulder in a space meant for peace, while an underlying tension in the environment never disappeared. Religious leaders and volunteers from outside are viewed as lifelines—outsiders who bring a small piece of the world inside. But the lines between genuine belief and self-preservation blur easily. Many women attend services not out of devotion but as an escape from the monotony of Camp, the absence of family, and the nagging guilt they're trying to get beyond. Unlike most places in the Camp, the chapel offers a reprieve from the ever-watchful eyes of guards. It's one of the few places where inmates can sit quietly, heads bowed in prayer, or simply seek solace in the silence.

Like everything else in Camp, faith comes with hierarchy. Women form informal cliques based on shared beliefs and friendships beyond the chapel. This is not unlike the power struggles found in any social group. Religious affiliation offers a shield against isolation for some, but it can also provoke jealousy and suspicion among others. Your position among the congregation can be like a form of currency—who sets the order of the program, who runs the choir, who runs bible studies, or religious movie nights. Having time to practice one's faith is often allowed more quickly than many other activities, so it is a powerful experience, and some try to use it for influence and position. Sadly, religion can be manipulated and used like any other program in the Camp. Those attending regularly don't take long to identify the underlying games or positioning. This hierarchy can be a source of comfort and community for some, but it can also be a source of tension and conflict for others.

For those who seek real transformation, however, maintaining faith in prison becomes an act of rebellion. Believing in something more significant, in a system that offers forgiveness, grace, or karmic justice, is its own kind of power. The penal system may try to strip these women of their humanity, but faith offers a way to reclaim it if your heart is in it. This is a powerful message of resilience and hope. For women who have faced abuse, addiction, or abandonment, religion can be the thread that ties them back to hope—however fragile it may seem.

But in the shadows of finding your faith lies doubt. Faith is not a shield from the violence, manipulation, and dehumanization that are ongoing in any prison system. Women pray fervently for deliverance and still find themselves returning to their cells with no promise of anything changing. In this way, religion in prison Camps is a delicate balance between hope and harsh reality.

And yet, for many, it is enough—enough to get through the day, find meaning in the chaos, and survive the uncertainty of what life on the inside brings. In the confines of the women's Camp, faith can bring solace, peace, and a time to search the inner demons of the mind. It can also provide a sense of purpose and order in an environment that often feels chaotic and unpredictable. With the support of volunteers and the Camp preacher, the weight of working through this process can be helped by bringing your religion to a more meaningful part of your ongoing life.

For those wanting to understand more about the role of faith in their lives, Camp is an excellent place to find its meaning. The library and the volunteers involved provide access to an abundance of materials. Rare is the woman who spends time in Camp who does not take time to do a little soul searching and coming to terms with their creator and life. When you find yourself in the depths of despair, singing along, finding an uplifting service, and sharing among those with a common belief are welcomed bright spots.

Chapter Twelve

THE RACE DIVIDE

While in prison, I was fortunate to work with the Big Sisters program. When the woman running the program was transferred, I was placed in charge, which opened my eyes to several aspects of prison life that are often left unsaid. One of the most prominent yet rarely discussed is the role race plays in prison dynamics. This reality might feel uncomfortable to talk about, but it's important to understand because it is a reality within the prison system, even in lower-security Camps.

Before entering prison, I spoke with a friend who had served time in a men's federal prison. He told me that someone from "my group" would approach me shortly after arrival to offer support and guidance. But when I arrived at the Camp, no one reached out. Initially, this confused me. During the pre-sentencing process, I had consistently listed my race as Hispanic, but officials kept changing it to Caucasian. I have no idea why. When I spent some time in the Camp, I realized the system, whether intentional or not, tends to categorize people based on their race. This separation wasn't as strict as in higher-security prisons, but it was still noticeable.

For example, at check-in, a black inmate working in Receiving and Delivery would often ensure that another black woman met and guided new arrivals of the same race. The role officially belonged to the Big Sisters program, but the racial dynamics were present, even in subtle ways. Over time, I came to understand that this was an unspoken part of how the system functioned. Different racial groups took care of themselves, offering support, clothing, and supplies to help new arrivals adjust.

It's important to emphasize that this was not inherently negative. In fact, the care and camaraderie shown by these groups provided a much-needed sense of family and security in an otherwise challenging environment. The women wanted to make sure their peers had a smoother transition. They often brought new arrivals to me so I could provide any extra supplies I had, ensuring fairness and transparency in the distribution.

Though these groups lived, ate, and participated in activities together, that didn't mean people of different races didn't interact. We all lived among one another, and while some friendships crossed racial lines, the initial sorting by race was a way people found comfort in a difficult situation.

Staff, too, displayed a degree of this dynamic. For instance, a black male warden was far more approachable to some of the black women than to me, which felt alienating at times. My dorm counselor, also a black man, would rush off when I approached but later warmed up when he took an interest in my husband's truck. The white staff, in contrast, often kept a distance from the inmates altogether, regardless of race.

Over time, I realized that the white women in the Camp did not seem to look out for each other in the same way the other racial groups did. They weren't as quick to form bonds, which could make being a white woman in prison feel isolating. The older white women, in particular, seemed to keep to themselves more, and this could make finding connections challenging.

However, this is not to say that friendships across racial lines didn't exist. Brenda, a Hispanic woman in my dorm, became a close friend despite pressure from some in her group to keep her distance from me. Her group didn't approve of our friendship, fearing it wouldn't last once we left prison. But we stayed close, proving that those barriers could be broken with effort and mutual respect.

One thing I learned during my time in prison is that building relationships takes time, trust, and patience. My bus stop housed younger women who didn't want an older woman around. But by sharing magazines, decorating our space, and being myself, I slowly gained their trust. Eventually, I earned the nickname "Biddy" and became friends with many of them. Over time, they even began to check in on me, asking if I was okay when someone new approached. This camaraderie, once built, became a source of support and protection.

Race is an undeniable factor in prison, but it doesn't have to define your entire experience. Over time, everyone finds their tribe, and this sense of community—whatever form it takes—can make a difficult situation more bearable. Navigating these dynamics with respect and openness can help you find your place and, ultimately, thrive despite the circumstances.

Chapter Thirteen

IT'S NO MICHELIN STAR

The good news is that a Cafeteria provides three meals a day. The bad news is that the food is not very good. Breakfast is served from 5:45 a.m. to around 8 a.m. It can be powdered eggs, rubbery pancakes, greasy baked bacon, boxes of cereal, yogurt, fruit, and some of the worst coffee I have ever had. The ladies were most excited when they served honey buns or freshly baked cinnamon rolls. This delicacy was rare but did occur. There are also boxes of juice and milk. The breakfast is not horrible, but it's nothing to get up early and race to eat.

Lunch starts at 10:00 a.m. and is wrapped up by 11:30 a.m. This schedule took some getting used to, as it seemed lunch came early. Lunch was predictable. There were hamburgers on Wednesdays and fish on Fridays. The fried chicken was good and served once a week, usually with boxed mashed potatoes and some vegetables. There was a salad bar for lunch and dinner, mostly lettuce with various salad dressings, sometimes cottage cheese. There was always a dessert. I felt the lunches were the best of the three meals, but it took a while to get used to eating lunch so early. You were typically done by 11 a.m.

Some lines form outside the cafeteria if it's nice or inside the dorms in lousy weather, waiting for the CO to announce the open line. There is a pecking order in the lines as well. If you work full-time, you can go to the front of the line. Everyone else fills in behind. As a town driver, I often asked if they would set lunch aside at breakfast as I may miss the time frame. I'm sure other jobs had to make special requests as well. There is always an apple or orange. The women liked to take these back to the rooms, but this could get you in trouble. The rule was that we could not take food out of the cafeteria.

Early dinner started from 3:00 p.m. The women liked to go to the early dinner before the 4:00 p.m. count because they might serve leftovers from lunch. Or if anything special was served, and a limited number of servings remained, it was first come, first serve.

The main dinner started once the 4:00 p.m. count was complete, and the cafeteria CO announced they were open. People would run to get in line, thinking they might run out of food. They might run out of the main course on rare occasions, but there would always be other options. I felt no meal prepared would excite me to run to get it. Some were better than others. Many nights, it seemed they were serving a mystery meat with rice or potatoes in a gravy or sauce.

Holiday meals were the best. They seemed more freshly prepared. They might serve stuffed peppers (everyone was excited to get the green peppers) or a better cut of beef for Christmas. There were typical holiday sides, and the portions were generous; the desserts were pieces of pumpkin pie. Especially with the holidays, if there was any food leftover and they announced "seconds," the women would run up to get more. As you leave the cafeteria on holidays, they hand you a sack lunch for your dinner for later. Again, these were "mystery meat" sandwiches, chips, fruit, and desserts. These would have to be taken to your room to eat as the cafeteria was closed for the evening meals on holidays. When you have visitors on a holiday, it depends on whether the CO will let you and a guest have a holiday meal together in the visitor's room. One of our CO's would never allow this; the other always did. If the CO didn't allow it, you missed out on that meal to have your visitor and had to settle for your sack lunch that hopefully someone collected for you. The cafeteria does make available meals for medically restricted diets, food allergies, and religious holidays.

It's not that the cafeteria didn't order fresh vegetables, but they were confiscated and sold to inmates out the backdoor of the warehouse before anyone even knew the product had arrived. This was obvious because women could be found cooking meals with their irons using peppers, onions, and other veggies when preparing their meals. The BOP meals must carry a specific nutritional value of protein, carbs, and a total calorie count per meal. Trust me, the better meals were found if you could line up with someone who would cook for you. Countless women rarely entered the cafeteria for a meal.

The alleys came alive every evening with the smell of prepared food. You could have a cup of cheesy noodles with tuna heated in it. Ladies knew how to make a variety of quesadillas, which were warm and delicious.

They also made enchiladas from scratch. A few women had contacts to get into the visitor's room and heat some of their meals using the microwave. Any of these meals were tasty with fresh onions and other vegetables mixed in, and again, the women were unbelievably creative with recipes. To participate in these meals, you had better have extra commissary funds and make friends with the various cooks.

Remember that these Camps are support systems for the federal prison associated with them. The main prison could be put in lockdown when in trouble. I saw them go into lockdown for a couple of weeks at times. During lockdowns, the men's cafeteria did not operate. The staff of the Camp cafeteria would be asked to prepare sack lunches to be provided to the main prison for as many as 1100 inmates. During this time, I and others preparing these lunches would be in the back around the food inventory and see food cans marked "not for human consumption."

That didn't sit well. The men's prison would need sack lunches to serve three times a day. If the lockdown lasted more than a couple of days, the COs would ask for volunteers to help prepare the voluminous amounts of sack lunches that were needed. Our reward for these efforts was a can of orange soda pop. The cafeteria still had to produce three meals daily for the women's Camp. I can't imagine eating a sack lunch for three meals a day. The hard part is, like anything, a few people would create the lockdown situation that everyone else would suffer through.

The cafeteria is a large room centered on the campus. While there needed to be more seating for the entire Camp to be there at once, there were a lot of seating arrangements with nice tables. I put in a "cop-out" request, a way to request something, complain, or snitch. I spoke to the cafeteria CO about why they didn't open the cafeteria between meals to allow the women to have another location to gather in small groups and mingle. The Camp is in desperate need of more locations for the women to gather and be able to get out of their rooms and the dorms. This reality is even more true in winter or bad weather when you can't go outside. The use of the cafeteria and the need for more benches were just two of the things that I never understood. It seemed like it would be so easy, but honestly, it was often a "not in my backyard" mentality. The cafeteria remained available for scheduled meals only.

Chapter Fourteen

YOU'VE GOT MAIL

Mail is a lifeline in prison—a vital connection to the outside world. Even sending a letter to yourself matters because it helps maintain that bridge beyond the walls. The types of mail allowed vary widely, often depending on the prison's recent experiences with contraband. If drugs were smuggled in, your mail privileges might be restricted, and during security incidents, there may even be temporary bans on mail. I've heard of fentanyl-laced into ink on postcards, creating chaos inside. These incidents do more than disrupt mail; they lead to lockdowns, medical emergencies, or even loss of good behavior credits. If enough people are affected, it could mean a lockdown for the entire Camp, making things tougher for everyone.

Here's What You Need to Know About Mail in Prison:

- **Hardcover Books:** Must be sent directly from Amazon
- **Softcover Books, Planners, Magazines, and Newspapers:** These can be sent by a business or by friends and family
- **Addressing Mail:** Be precise and include "Camp satellite" in the address

- **Contraband Concerns:** Stickers, glitter, or any loose items are considered contraband
- **Photos:** You can have up to 25 pictures at a time
- **Blank Cards and Paper:** Any blank materials for personal use must have something written in pencil; you can erase and reuse it later
- **Postage Costs:** There's a 30% markup on postage, so a single card could cost up to $4 to mail
- **Legal Mail:** If labeled "attorney-client privilege," the guards won't open it

At my Camp, there was a mail call every weekday evening in the visitor's room after dinner. Even if you're not expecting anything, you're required to attend. But when you are getting a piece of mail, even just a postcard, it is nice. Let your friends and family know that every letter counts. Over time, those who initially wrote to you may stop, so be prepared to keep communication alive by writing back. It's comforting to know they remember you, especially as time passes.

Everyone dreads Contraband Tuesdays. It starts with a 5:30 a.m. wake-up call over the PA system, followed by the officer announcing the names of those who have received contraband mail. I ended up on the list often enough that everyone at Camp knew who I was. My friend's kids sent cards with stickers, which were deemed contraband. The officer at the admin office would sometimes call out offenders multiple times if they didn't arrive fast enough, and once there, he'd inform you—loudly and publicly—that your mail was being thrown out. It's frustrating, especially when you know your loved ones just wanted to brighten your day.

Thankfully, I received a lot of mail while I was there. My husband ensured it, even recruiting friends on Facebook to send cards and letters. Some women had "mail envy" (except on those early Contraband Tuesdays), but I shared everything. By Halloween, I had enough cards to decorate our bus stop, and for Christmas, I covered the entire top ledge of our alley with cards and decorations. We weren't technically supposed to, but it brought a bit of holiday cheer into our world. We all loved decorating, and everyone came in to enjoy them—even the guards.

Remember, those in charge will inspect anything you send or receive, so be mindful of what you share. Personal or financial details are likely to be read by guards, and you need someone on the outside handling your matters to avoid this. Staying connected is crucial, especially considering how fast the world changes. For those inside, mail can be a vital thread back to a world they'll eventually rejoin.

Preparing for Camp: About ten days before you self-surrender, mail yourself some essentials: crossword books, softcover reading material, a list of contacts, restitution documents, and any legal papers, including a simple will and medical directives. Make sure your return address is clear and follows the correct format. Here's an example based on my experience:

Send to:

> #26542-045
> FCI Greenville
> Federal Correction Institution
> Satellite Camp
> PO Box 6000
> Greenville, Illinois 62246.

> "HOLD FOR
> V CHERYL WOMACK
> SELF SURRENDER ON
> JULY 17, 2017"

This step ensures you'll have everything you need on arrival, and it's comforting to receive something on that first day—even if it's a letter from yourself. You can call the Camp prior to arrival to confirm they have received your package.

Chapter Fifteen

ED-DUH-CATION

As one of the women who had the opportunity to teach in the GED classes and an entrepreneur class for night programming, I have so much to say about the education system within the prison. I can only speak personally from my Camp and from the input the women attending classes in other institutions shared with me.

First and most importantly, if you don't have your High School Diploma, you will need to get your GED. It might be court-ordered, and the BOP requires you to attend these classes and continue taking the test until you pass. You can lose good time if you miss these classes or tests. You'll take math, literature, social studies, geography, history, and science courses.

The first thing I immediately noticed when teaching social studies, was that many women struggled because they didn't understand the meaning of the words used in the test questions. Typically, an instructor would sit in and read along as inmates reviewed the books provided. Sometimes, the inmates would have to read the books themselves. The problem is that you need to understand the words or the context of the questions to give the correct answer. In my classes I used index cards to list unfamiliar words with their definitions on the back to help them comprehend their meaning. In each class, we added new words and reviewed the flashcards.

Keep in mind that both the books and GED tests used in prison needs to be updated. We used books from the late 1990s, even though I was teaching in 2017. If you don't pass your GED while in Camp, you'll need to continue classes after your release while under BOP supervision or if court ordered. The information and GED questions could differ and be more current when you're out of prison.

Instructors also have different teaching styles. You'll be dealing with a lot of egos. I didn't account for this; it came back to bite me. One instructor complained to the CO that I was "teaching" too much, thinking that I should just read the material. However, my approach was hands-on to help inmates grasp the information. I encourage you to be honest with your instructor—if you don't understand something, ask. They get paid regardless, but it's important to *you* to grasp the material, advance to other courses, and pass the test.

We also created flashcards to review the Bill of Rights since the test often summarized them in multiple-choice questions. You need to know them to answer correctly. If your instructor doesn't do this, try making your own cards. Many women passed the test successfully using these methods. An index card for any term explicitly covered in the test can be helpful. For example, if you don't understand the word "explicitly," you'll struggle to apply reason and answer appropriately (now you know why I had my husband send me bulk index cards).

Other courses follow a similar format: You need to master the basics before moving to more advanced work.

There's also an order in which you'll take the classes. Ideally, you'll start with literature and social science, as they're easier and help familiarize you with the types of test questions you'll encounter.

Evening programs, following the typical semester schedule, are also available. Any woman can submit a plan to teach a class based on her hobbies or skills, and you might be one of them. You'll lay out a plan for a ten-week course and submit it to the CO over-seeing education. If approved, inmates can sign up for this class. These classes range from studying the planets to crochet, entrepreneurship, or parenting (part of the RDAP program, which I'll cover later). At least 10 women must sign up for the class to proceed.

It's a good idea to sign up for these classes for several reasons: they make time pass more quickly, introduce you to new people, and you might learn something valuable. You also earn certificates, which can be beneficial when you're released. These certificates go into your inmate file and can help you get into a better halfway house or even transfer from a higher-security prison to a Camp. Consider teaching a class to expose others to new things if you have a particular skill. Creating structure in your days and nights helps time pass faster.

The GED program provides a solid foundation. The "DUH" in the title refers to the outdated material and the possible necessity of self-teaching due to unengaged instructors. This fact frustrates me. The head correctional officer managing the education department should take their role seriously. Their success is measured by how many women sign up for the test and how many pass. It frustrates me when I see minimal effort from the top to encourage hands-on, effective teaching. I brought in the *Wall Street Journal* to discuss current congressional bills, connecting what we learned in class about how a bill becomes law with real-life applications. What better way to remember?

I recently read that a women's prison in Kansas partnered with a university to offer college courses through Zoom at no cost. You can also apply to take mail-in college courses at your expense. I love the idea of adding education to your resume while serving time—these courses could be the start of something transformative. Some prisons even offer cosmetology programs, another great opportunity to start a new career. It's the perfect time to seize these opportunities and make the most of a difficult situation. Continuous learning is an example of *you* doing the time, not letting the time do you.

Chapter Sixteen
CROSSING THE TRACKS: RDAP

The Federal Bureau of Prisons established the Residential Drug Abuse Program (RDAP) in 1989, aiming to help individuals address substance abuse issues while offering a chance for reduced sentencing. Authorized by 18 U.S. Code § 3621(e)(2)(B), RDAP is the only BOP program through which individuals serving federal sentences can earn time off their sentences. For those who complete the program, there's the potential to receive up to a one-year sentence reduction and an additional six-month placement in a halfway house or home confinement to support a smoother reintegration.

RDAP is a structured program with multiple phases generally conducted in a designated dorm area. Participants must meet certain requirements, including having a history of substance abuse or dependency and serving a nonviolent offense sentence. The program involves 500 hours of intensive substance abuse treatment, with individualized plans supervised by a Drug Treatment Specialist. Through these phases, RDAP aims to help participants build coping skills and prepare for their return to society.

In practice, however, RDAP can be quite different from what one might expect. At our Camp, the RDAP dorm felt almost like a separate world. The participants lived, ate, and worked out together, mostly separate from the rest of the Camp. Many of us found this odd, as you would think preparation for the real world would involve more interaction with different types of people. Unfortunately, the program at my Camp seemed more like a cult to some rather than a supportive community focused on recovery.

The strict structure imposed on participants included a rigorous daily routine, beginning at 5 a.m. They had to adhere to stringent rules regarding their appearance and conduct. Each day, they were subject to "group assessments," where participants received feedback—sometimes harshly critical—from their peers. I frequently encountered women who came to my class visibly shaken from these sessions, recounting the emotional toll of standing in front of the group to hear every perceived flaw dissected. Despite the intention for this to be constructive, it often left them distressed.

This group is preyed on from all angles. It starts with advertisements from attorneys to desperate women trying to find a way to reduce their time. The unscrupulous attorney or specialist will charge these women more than $10,000 assuring them entry into this program and more time off. When in fact they have nothing to do with the BOP and are in no position to make these guarantees.

In addition to these challenges, the women in that program had to carefully monitor their actions and friendships. Even a perceived connection with someone from outside the RDAP dorm could result in disciplinary action. Maintaining friendships was difficult in this environment, as participants were unsure who they could trust. The stakes were high, with even minor infractions leading to expulsion from the program, often near the end, when they had invested months into trying to earn time off their sentence.

While some managed to thrive, many others struggled, navigating an environment rife with backstabbing and constant surveillance. Some women shared stories of having to wait months just to enter the program due to overcrowding, all the while enduring the mental strain of hoping for an early release. It was a mixed experience for those involved; for some, it felt more like a test of endurance than a path to recovery.

However, there were moments of growth and transformation that I found rewarding to witness. A correctional officer once told me that people who fall into substance abuse often find their emotional development arrested at the age they began using. It helped me relate to some of the younger women in the program as I watched them begin to mature and grow in ways they hadn't before. When they trusted and engaged with the process, you could see changes unfolding before your eyes. As a teacher and occasional driver for medical visits/appointments, I saw firsthand the resilience and potential within these women, which filled me with empathy and hope for their futures.

I don't want to criticize RDAP because its intent is positive, and it's a nationwide program that has helped many. My experience at our Camp, however, left me wishing for greater oversight and support for the women involved. If you find yourself entering RDAP, I hope your experience will be filled with encouragement, connection, and true recovery. I hope you encounter other strong women striving to overcome their pasts and become the remarkable people they were meant to be.

Chapter Seventeen

YOUR HEALTH, YOUR BURDEN

Once you process through Receiving and Delivery, you'll go to Medical. You'll make several visits initially as they establish a baseline of your health. Remember, you are the key player in your healthcare system until you're out of Camp and in a halfway house. Hopefully, you've already sent yourself a list of your current medications in your original package and a completed medical directive form (see the back of this book under Resources). Make sure to include precise information on medication names, doses, and frequency to ensure you get what you need.

One crucial step is finding a trustworthy contact within the Camp to share information with about your emergency contact on the outside. If a medical emergency occurs, the Camp will not notify your family, but you can ensure someone has your emergency contact information. This and the medical directive are essential steps to take for your peace of mind. It's up to you to develop your support system within the Camp.

If you're allowed to keep your medications with you, you'll receive a 30-day supply and can refill them through the TRULINCS system (where you'll also access emails). You can request refills via the "refills" tab. If you're required to go to "pill call," expect to line up multiple times a day to receive medications under supervision. Diabetic inmates will go to a "diabetic call." You'll need to take your medication in front of the nurse, show you've swallowed it, and drink water.

Medical care at Camp includes a full-time PRN and another nurse, with a visiting community dentist coming in weekly. Mornings offer a short, 15-minute window for those who need immediate care, and a similar window is available weekly for dental issues. These are usually triage appointments, with further treatments arranged as needed through "call-outs." As the town driver, I often took women for off-site treatments, like outpatient surgeries, x-rays, and rehab.

One challenging aspect is the delay in receiving test results. You might have an x-ray or MRI and then wait months for results. Discrepancies between outside doctors and Camp doctors are common; unfortunately, you have little say in your treatment. Keeping a copy of any outside medical notes is wise, as it could offer some recourse later. You can make copies with a copy card purchased from the commissary and keep these copies with your legal records.

One particularly poignant case involved a woman waiting months for a breast lump diagnosis. The delay continued through multiple transfers and resulted in a late-stage cancer diagnosis. Her journey and eventual passing highlighted the slow process and the emotional toll it can take on everyone involved. This experience underscored the importance of health and self-care, especially for those of us at an older age.

As the town driver, I suggested group mammogram appointments to increase inmate access to this essential care. We'd load up the van twice a month and head to the medical facility. While this was sometimes logistically challenging, the arrangement allowed more women to access preventive care. However, the importance of following the rules cannot be overstated, as any infraction, like one inmate caught smoking can lead to serious consequences. It could even result in the termination of this program.

Camp medical care can be challenging, especially after outpatient procedures. Recovery takes place in a standard bunk with no special accommodations. If you need follow-up care, you must take yourself to Medical, even if you are using crutches or a wheelchair, as nurses don't make dorm visits.

Dental and vision care can be particularly daunting. Women recovering from drug use, especially meth, often need extensive dental work, including dentures, which can take over a year to receive. Delays are common, as are cases of ill-fitting dentures requiring replacements. Similarly, vision issues may require long waits for corrective eyewear.

Lastly, as a town driver, I've observed that many women, especially those who've been institutionalized for years, find navigating a medical facility intimidating. I always stayed with them to ensure they received the support they needed. When the nurse or doctor gave me instructions, I would carefully note the details to ensure their care would continue smoothly back at Camp.

Remember, while the Camp's medical system has its challenges, focusing on preventive care and minimizing medical visits, when possible, can make a big difference.

Take responsibility for your health, stay vigilant, and don't hesitate to advocate for yourself whenever possible. By staying proactive, you can manage your health and maximize your available resources, even in the face of these challenges.

Chapter Eighteen

EVERYONE DOES THE TIME

From the moment this process begins, moving you toward incarceration, I promise this is not happening only to you. Your family and friends feel your fear, pain, frustration, sadness, anger, and every other emotion you're experiencing. They also carry these feelings but may not know how to express them as they try to protect you from additional worry. But they can see and feel everything you're going through. I wish I had spent more time discussing these feelings—and theirs—while this was happening.

Your loved ones need help explaining the situation to their friends, schools, employers, and other families. A gentle conversation about how they feel could make a big difference in helping them cope and, in turn, help you both through the experience. I wish I had taken more time to help my sons understand what was happening and how I managed it, to give them pointers for themselves. My sons are grown, but I can only imagine how difficult this must be for younger children. My kids heard smug and snarky remarks from so-called friends. It's vital to keep in touch with your kids—at any age—to know what they're hearing and help them deal with and respond to it. For younger children, meeting with their teacher or principal is essential. By making yourself vulnerable and approachable, you help others handle things more kindly.

Believe it or not, the more you talk about it, the easier the situation becomes. I'm not saying the pain and discomfort will disappear, but life becomes a little easier when you learn to speak openly about what's happening. While this experience is temporary, it will forever impact your life.

Sadly, more people are going to prison than ever before. While I don't want to normalize it, we must stop stigmatizing it. It takes all of us to accept mistakes and move forward, allowing those involved to find their way again. But, if no one knows, or people are shocked when they find out you're going to or have been in prison, it becomes harder for everyone. I've had countless conversations with contractors, business associates, and friends, and I openly share my pain and my desire to live a normal life. What continues to surprise me is that most of them almost always know someone who's been incarcerated—or they've done time themselves—and never felt comfortable sharing it. They lower their heads as they tell you, expecting judgment, even though you just told them you've been in prison. I once shared my story with a young sales clerk, who then meekly confided that his father was in jail. He must have felt relieved to tell someone. While this isn't a badge of honor, it's something you carry with you for the rest of your life.

Now, let's talk about how to stay in touch while you're serving time. Leave some self-addressed envelopes or postcards with younger family members, and ask them to send a picture they drew or a short note from time to time. Make it as easy as possible for them to communicate with you. If they're over 12, ensure they're listed on your pre-sentencing report so they can easily visit if funds allow. If travel is an issue, schedule video chats. While they cost a little more (around $6.00 each), they last 25 minutes, and you can see each other. The video chats are through the TRULINK system, where you can schedule up to three at a time. A calendar shows available times; you need three full days' notice before scheduling. You must wear your prison-issued green dress shirt and lanyard to appear fully dressed for the call. If you miss your scheduled time, you will be charged even if the call doesn't happen. Try to schedule calls for the same time each week, so you're more likely to remember. Also, be aware that these chats, like everything else, are monitored, and you can lose good time for breaking rules—like inappropriate behavior, sharing the call with another inmate, or having a group call from the other side of the video chat.

You can find a children's book *Mommy Loves You Everywhere* through the Women of Worth website (www.womenofworthwow.org), where your family can read a warm story of love from mother to child, beautifully illustrated with real scenes inside a Camp. It shows them how you dress, how you might work, and what the phones or computers look like. These small things are helpful to share, especially with younger children. Take time to write short notes. If you have more time, write several at once, sharing your daily events or thoughts, and then send them out gradually. Don't send everything at once—being consistent in your involve-ment helps children feel your presence even while you're away.

Ask your loved ones for details about how they're spending their time. Are they seeing friends? How is school? Can you talk about the house pets? Discussing everyday things helps normalize their lives—and that's what you're striving for. Be sure to ask what's hard for them right now and give them space to share those struggles. While this is hard for all of you, they need to know that you're doing everything possible to remain part of their lives. It takes some planning. I've seen par-ents use video chat to FaceTime during a graduation or other special celebration. Your connection with your family will be as much about what you choose to make of it. Staying physically and mentally present is crucial, even from a distance.

If you're married, your spouse carries a much larger burden. It's important to give them as much support as possible, understand their challenges, and encourage them through this process. Being away from your fam-ily and life is hard, but imagine how hard it is for them to deal with your absence. From my own experience, I took the approach I was the one in prison, and everyone should pity me. The problem with this type of thinking is when you finally return to your home, your partner may have had their fill of taking care of everything, and now that you are out and they consider you safe—they may decide life will be easier without you in it.

I watched this happen on several occasions. While you try to adjust to your new life in prison, they are still juggling everything on the outside. Not only do they have to continue with daily life, but they also have to pick up the slack where you once helped—financially and emotionally. They are dealing with other friends and family who might not be nice about this situation. With children, especially young ones, you have to try and explain the situation to their teachers, friends, parents, schools, and more.

It's not easy. The more you can appreciate and support their extra efforts, the less likely you'll face resentment when you return. They aren't you and won't handle everything the way you would—let it go and be grateful someone is there, trying to hold it all together. On the flip side of this, you may decide while you are away, that you have outgrown the relationship and find yourself unwilling to stay in it when you return. Time can change everything. I'm not saying it's not for the better. Still, all of you will be dealing with changes in attitudes, relationships, and friendships, and you will continue to deal with the guilt of putting your family in these circumstances. Going to prison and being part of the penal system has far-reaching tentacles.

Some women choose not to have their children visit while they're in prison. If you can afford it, even occasional visits are important. That face-to-face time is precious. It lets you see how your kids are doing and reassures them that you're okay. When my oldest son first visited, he made me look him in the eye and tell him I was okay. I hadn't realized until that moment just how afraid he had been for me. Those visits, though rare, bonded us and kept our lines of communication open.

It's easy to dwell on the birthdays, holidays, graduations, parties, and trips you're missing. But remember, your loved ones are losing time with *you* during these moments, too. They may not voice it, but they're hurting just as much as you are. When you do time, so do they—on many different levels.

Chapter Nineteen

WHATEVER CAN GO WRONG, WILL GO WRONG

This chapter reminds you that nothing ever goes as planned, so be prepared for the unexpected. While you may have spent a good deal of time trying to plan for all of the contingencies that might come up while incarcerated. The reality is that life will happen despite the best planning. I have personal circumstances and friends' stories to share.

A couple of weeks after incarceration, my son told me the bank demanded we move all our business accounts and mortgages to another bank. I was in prison and away from the real world. I had set aside 10 minutes a day of phone time to talk to family. I had been with this bank for twenty years, and had a large sum of cash in my accounts. I had been going through this legal process for nine years, and NOW they wanted me to move my business. I was shocked and upset. It fell on my son's shoulders, who had never managed these things before, to find a bank to take our business and assume our mortgage. He was overwhelmed, and I was distressed at the limited amount I was able to help.

When it was time for my home and auto insurance renewal, I found that the insurance company would not renew my business because of my conviction. I was fortunate to have an insurance agent who worked with my son to find a policy that would cost more, but still provide the necessary coverage. I gave my son an executed power of attorney so he was able to handle these types of matters in my absence.

On more than one occasion, I had women come to me and ask if they could send my husband their bank statements to keep them in safe hands. Unfortunately, in many cases, their family was involved in drugs, and they figured out how to access the women's money and use it for their purposes.

My friend planned to return to her home upon release. Sadly, the property was raided and then abandoned while she was incarnated and was no longer livable. I have heard stories of homes burning down or going into foreclosure. There are so many unknowns to manage that there are simply no guarantees. These are the kinds of things where I suggest you realize if it can go wrong, it will.

I became a town driver a few months into my time at Camp. I learned how to schedule video chats in advance with my son. Suddenly, I found myself on the road, traveling unexpectedly and away from the Camp. From personal experience, I know there is no feeling worse than to sit at the end of a video chat and have the other party be a "no-show." It is emotionally devastating.

On one of my son's birthdays, I fell ill with a very bad bug and lost my voice. On his birthday, I always called him. Remember I told you to make calls after you put your information into the phone; you must say your name and be voice recognized. With my horse-whispering voice, that was not going to happen. It was the first and only time I would miss his birthday. All I could do was lay in bed and cry.

I planned to have money on my books and be ready to visit with my husband the first weekend. I arrived on the Thursday before a holiday weekend. Even though I was there by 11 a.m. for a report time of 2 p.m., the medical department had emergencies, and I got held up in processing until the 4 p.m. count. Everything that connects you to the world is processed and turned on at the main FCI. The commissary closed on Thursday, so I missed the chance to buy general hygiene products or casual clothes. My dorm counselor had also taken the long weekend off, so he could not approve visits from people listed in my pre-sentencing report – like my husband. Though we had planned to see each other that first weekend, I had to find someone to call their husband to tell my husband he was not going to be able to visit. We were both devastated, but these were the hands we were dealt.

Life doesn't stop for your family and friends on the outside. No matter how well you plan, unforeseen circumstances can disrupt your communication and visitation plans. I've witnessed women making call after call, trying to reach their loved ones with no success. It's a stark reminder of the importance of communication and the challenges that can arise when it's disrupted. These inconsistencies can be particularly difficult for younger children, and it's crucial to remember that unexpected changes in plans can occur beyond your control.

Remember, when you are in a bus stop or a group setting, if one person does something wrong, you can all be part of the punishment. Life is not fair, and that doesn't change just because you are somewhere with a lot of rules.

Who knew that the FCI could lock down the FCP when fog set in? When that happens, no one is allowed to come or go. This means if your family or a friend traveled a long distance at great expense to visit, they wouldn't get in until the lockdown is lifted if they were able to get in at all. These are heart-wrenching to both the visitors and the inmates. It is common to arrive in the visiting room and find that some of the vending machines are empty. That may not seem like a big deal, but it can be if you are there for six-plus hours with nothing to eat or drink, especially if you have kids visiting.

One woman in Camp was punished for a crime she and her husband committed jointly. They agreed he would stay home and raise their son, and she would take the fall. By the time she got out, he had filed for divorce and full custody of the child because she was now a felon. She left everything with him for the benefit of her child, and now she lost everything.

If you are involved in a crime with co-defendants, you will learn that any two of you cannot serve time in the same prison. If the other person arrives at the Camp first, you will probably be sent to a different location. If several people are involved, it might take a few locations and several moves to a place where you can stay. This is very unsettling, as the travel from one prison location to another is anything but pleasant and safe. You have no control over your future location, belongings, or transfer date.

If you get called as a cooperating witness for a trial, you can be removed at the will of the judicial system, where you will end up in a County or City jail for an undetermined amount of time. Your personal possessions are put in storage with no guarantee you will get all of these back, and you lose your bedding placement. With all the routines of prison life, if these types of things happen, your life is thrown into upheaval, and you have to start again.

A bunkie of mine spent over $10,000 with an alleged attorney to assure her she would get into the RDAP program, where she could earn an additional year off for good behavior and get out sooner. She didn't qualify, and if he was a legitimately trained attorney, he should have known. She was cheated out of a lot of money. No one can guarantee your placement in any BOP programs before you arrive.

The takeaway from this chapter is to prepare yourself and your family and friends to realize that whatever can go wrong will go wrong. You need to keep an open mind about the unexpected.

Chapter Twenty

READY OR NOT

When your release date is approaching, a Case Manager will work with the BOP to help you transition to the next phase of reentry. Their job is to coordinate your placement at a halfway house, setting a date for your release. For me, one of the most complex parts of going to Camp was the uncertainty of when and how I'd be getting out. Unfortunately, some Case Managers let the power of this process go to their heads, and reliable information can be scarce. Often, rumors fill the gaps, leading to confusion and anxiety about what comes next. Even when you receive your proposed out-date, you may not know exactly where you're headed or when, leaving you in constant limbo as you try to plan for the future.

As more halfway houses close across the U.S., you could face delays due to limited space. Once your Case Manager submits the application, the halfway house has to confirm availability. If there's no room, you might end up staying longer at Camp, which is particularly disappointing for those who've completed programs like RDAP to earn early release.

Occasionally, a group of professionals who work with halfway houses will come to Camp to provide some insights. The main takeaway from my meeting was that halfway houses are under increasing budget constraints, which makes placements even more uncertain. Without consistent, accurate information, many of us had to rely on advice from other women who had been through the process. It's frustrating to piece together what you need to know from secondhand sources rather than a reliable authority.

Getting your official out date is a big deal. Just as important as getting this date is to avoid bragging or **even** talking about it. When I thought I knew my out date, I spoke to my roommate, and unbeknownst to me a woman on the other side of the wall was listening. She turned me in to the Case Manager when I had not been formally notified of my date. I was estimating the date on my calendar with no official input. While you think this is not a big deal, this can promote feelings of jealousy or sadness in other inmates. Some women won't be getting out for a very long time. My Case Manager pulled my paperwork and wouldn't work on my case even though what he was told was a rumor, not factual. I have seen women lose their out-date from this kind of casual bragging. Just don't talk about it.

Everyone has an official release date from the BOP, which includes time spent at the halfway house. Although the BOP oversees halfway houses, you'll begin working with the judicial system again to manage parole and plan your life post-release. I was given the option to stay at Camp as a town driver for an extra 30 days, which felt safer than being in a halfway house with 185 other people, mostly men. These are the types of choices you'll need to consider as you prepare for reentry.

A sign that things are moving forward is when your family tells you that someone from the BOP and Office of Probation has inspected where you plan to live after the halfway house. Having a stable place to live is essential, but reentry comes with its challenges. As a felon, you'll likely face difficulties finding housing and may even have trouble opening a bank account. While more employers are willing to hire felons, your options may still be limited based on the nature of your offense. Insurance will likely be more expensive, and your employment prospects might narrow.

For example, my bank of 20 years closed my account after my conviction, and my insurance company only offered high-risk coverage with hefty premiums. This reality is why I advised earlier not to keep rental property or a mortgaged home, as the journey to rebuild your life will be full of challenges. Before you go to the halfway house is the time to start planning: Where will you live? Will you need an ankle monitor, and what are the associated costs? What kind of work can you realistically pursue? How will you get to the Federal Probation Office, and do you have reliable transportation?

You may not have all the answers until you're in the halfway house. Sometimes, your halfway house is far from where you used to live, which may require finding temporary work and housing until you're fully released. Once you secure employment, you can look for a permanent place to live. Before moving in, a Federal Probation Officer will need to approve your housing, and they'll conduct occasional checks when settled.

Inmates often say you can't have a cell phone, but you'll quickly find that you need one so the authorities can reach you. With so much conflicting information, the process can feel confusing and unsettling. I found this phase of transition to be one of the most uncertain.

As you prepare to leave Camp, ensure your paperwork is in order. Have copies of all legal documents, certificates, and proof of any educational achievements like your GED. Your Federal Probation Officer may need these, and if you don't bring proof, they'll have to request it from the BOP, which can take time. I once met someone who had to attend GED classes even though she'd completed the program simply because the documentation wasn't available. Make things easier by keeping organized copies with you.

Upon leaving Camp, you'll visit the main FCI facility to sign paperwork and collect any remaining money. These funds come on a JP Morgan debit card with your prison photo and ID number. If someone is picking you up, they need pre-approval to transport you, and you'll have a strict timeframe to reach the halfway house. If no one can pick you up, the town driver will take you to the nearest bus station and provide a one-way ticket to your new location, where a town driver or a U.S. Marshal will meet you.

Before you go to Camp—or once you're there—it's crucial to confirm you have no outstanding warrants. I've seen women get ready to leave, only to find out they had unresolved charges that required transfer to another prison. If you have any pending charges, address them while in Camp. Your lawyer can work on this so that a judge might consider the time served as fulfilling any additional sentences. Before releasing your attorney, have them check for outstanding warrants at all levels—city, county, and state. This review is vital information to keep on hand.

Chapter Twenty-one
HALFWAY—BUT NOT HOME

At age 67, I was assigned to a halfway house in Leavenworth, Kansas, after the closer Kansas City location shut down. My husband looked up the rules and information about the place for me. The halfway house was more like a large commercial building located in front of a state prison.

Inside was an entry with a check-in window and a locked door leading to the interior. Several dorm areas housed both men and women; out of 185 inmates, only 17 were women. What unsettled me most was the lack of locks on any doors beyond the entry. Now, I was living with a diverse group of people, including those convicted of serious offenses. The setup included a kitchen, meeting rooms, and offices for the two counselors. Residents were required to take a urine test whenever you returned from outside.

Within your first few days at the halfway house, you'll meet with a parole supervisor, who will review your record from Camp and assign your Federal Probation Officer. Depending on your progress, these start as in-person visits and eventually transition to phone check-ins.

The halfway house doesn't provide essentials like work clothes or a winter coat, so you'll need to take care of these on your own. I donated a couple of winter coats while I was there, as it was November and the temperatures were dropping. Nearby thrift stores are great places to find affordable clothing and other necessities. Although space is limited like it was at Camp, the rules are less strict about keeping everything put away. Still, I found it wise to keep my belongings secure.

Not everything you bring from Camp may be allowed here, so be prepared for a thorough search of your belongings upon arrival. Each halfway house has its own set of rules, and it's helpful to familiarize yourself with them early on.

You'll meet with an assigned counselor to discuss employment opportunities and the expected length of your stay, which could be up to a year. Due to limited halfway house spaces, especially for women, turnover is often quick. At this location, only one of 14 dorms was allocated for women, which reflects the overall demand.

The counselors manage large caseloads and are often overwhelmed, so it helps to be proactive. Make a list of questions or items you need, like forms for outside activities, and stay organized. Taking initiative can ease the process and help you feel more in control. It's tempting to wait to be told what to do, but being gently proactive will smooth your path.

This was my first experience with 10-minute walks, which are common in higher-security facilities. An announcement is made at the top of every hour, allowing you 10 minutes to reach your destination. Wherever you are at the end of those 10 minutes, you stay until the next hour.

The halfway house environment can feel chaotic at times. With so many people moving around, it's common to witness fights or confrontations. This can be unsettling, but remember to stay focused and centered. Lockdowns happen regularly, where you'll need to stay in your dorm. If you're not working, these days can feel particularly long.

Classes at the halfway house are limited. They offer orientation for newcomers, and some classes focus on drug education. Since that wasn't relevant to me, I didn't participate, but job postings are available on a bulletin board in the lunchroom. Demonstrating an active job search is important to your eventual release. If you have the funds, you can order food for delivery, which adds a bit of normalcy.

It's essential to handle all forms and approvals proactively. You submit a form which includes a time line of all your activities for day, night, or weekend release. This is very detailed and includes name of location, times, and who you will be affiliating with. If you do not follow your approved form exactly, you will be in violation and could go back to Camp. Your Counselor will check locations and make calls to confirm you are where you say you are. Keep extra forms on hand; the approval process can take a few days. Always ensure the front desk has a copy of your approved requests.

The rules remain strict, and you manage schedules to keep activities separate from the men. You can schedule trips to shop for necessities, attend job interviews, and meet with family. Transportation options are usually nearby; if you have access to a car, you'll need to get it registered and approved by the facility.

Living quarters are similar to Camp, with metal beds and plastic mattresses. As I was retired, I didn't need to find a job, but for those who aren't retired securing employment is required before you can move on to independent housing. When that time comes, remember that housing options might be limited, as some complexes don't rent to those with a record. Smaller complexes, townhouses, or duplexes offer better prospects.

Chapter Twenty-two

WALKING THE PROBATION TIGHTROPE

One of the first things to be aware of is that once you leave the BOP, your medical coverage ends. This is the time to start shopping for coverage. The Affordable Care Act was designed to provide more accessible benefits for situations like this, so look into available plans to help you at this stage. If you're of retirement age or were already on Social Security before entering prison, you must visit your local Social Security office to reinstate your benefits.

They will verify your prison entry date and adjust your payments. For example, I was paid for the first two months of incarceration, so they withheld payments for two months after my release to balance the overpayment. To reinstate your benefits, you need to visit your local Social Security office and provide them with your prison entry date. They will then adjust your payments accordingly. Don't assume these benefits will automatically restart – take proactive steps to ensure they do.

While living in a halfway house has challenges, returning to your home can also bring a new set of adjustments. During this time, you're transitioning from the BOP to the judicial system. Some parolees will have an ankle monitor with restrictions, costs, and specific rules. Everything—appointments, jobs, church, even grocery shopping—must be pre-approved, and you'll be given a timeframe to complete each task. Be sure to save every email request you make and approval you receive, just in case there's a change in your Federal Probation Officer or any misunderstandings.

Federal Probation Officers can visit anytime and expect you to show them around your residence. If you have an ankle monitor, you'll need to check in with them in person, and their surprise visits will likely be more frequent.

From your pre-sentencing report, you'll know the length of your parole. As your parole draws to a close, go through a checklist of expectations to complete the process. Your final check-in will include a visit to your home, where they'll confirm that you've met all the conditions tied to your sentence. For instance, I needed to submit financial updates and tax returns throughout my parole period.

You must submit a budget to your Federal Probation Officer for approval if you owe restitution. They'll review your expenses and determine what portion of your income goes toward restitution. For example, while they may allow you to attend a family wedding in another city, they might not approve transportation funds. It can be tricky, so working cooperatively with them is essential. Any travel across the state line or beyond your designated mileage must be approved in advance and in writing. When traveling, keep this authorization approval with you at all times. You'll be happy you have this if you get stopped for any reason.

Eventually, you'll transition from in-person visits to weekly phone check-ins. You'll be asked standard questions about your living situation, travel, and any new residents in your home. Keeping up with these calls is essential; failure to do so can result in a return to in-person visits, so stay on top of them.

Adjusting to a life of decision-making after years of following orders can be challenging. Being 'institutionalized' means you're used to someone else's direction and may feel out of your depth when faced with choices. This transition period is about rebuilding that decision-making muscle and learning to navigate options independently, often for the first time in a while. It's important to recognize this feeling and work on developing your own decision-making skills.

Probation means you're now under the judicial system, and any rule violations can result in being sent back to prison. Stories of people being re-incarcerated for minor infractions are unfortunately common, so adhere to the rules diligently. Avoid situations that might jeopardize your progress, and steer clear of others who are also on parole, as they can sometimes complicate your path forward.

This is also a crucial time to rebuild your life thoughtfully. If you've struggled with addiction, you may be required to participate in a rehabilitation program. Remember to set boundaries with family and friends who might still be using. If a family member struggles with addiction, be cautious about letting them live with you, as this can lead to further complications and even the possibility of re-incarceration. I knew one woman who let her daughter move in, and when authorities suspected the daughter of drug activity, they raided the property. As drugs were found on the premises my friend was sent back to prison. You've spent years preparing for this moment, so put those hard-won skills to use by surrounding yourself with supportive people and creating a healthy environment.

The financial aspect of this journey may also be complex, especially if you owe restitution. The government will allocate what they believe is reasonable from your income, and you'll need to make do with what remains.

If you sold your car or home before entering prison, you may have some funds saved to help with this fresh start. Top priorities should be securing a safe place to live and a reliable vehicle. Rebuilding from scratch can be daunting, especially with the stigma of a criminal record. Some women have found that starting over on their own—whether financially or with new social connections—is the best path forward, even if it means leaving some family relationships behind.

Chapter Twenty-three
THE HAMSTER WHEEL

After years of following others' orders and having decisions made for you, reentering society can feel overwhelming. Suddenly, you're expected to create a plan, make decisions, and take action after being told what to do for so long. You may find yourself institutionalized by prison life—used to someone else's rules and routines, making navigating the many choices ahead daunting. Life outside isn't black and white, and having so many options can be stressful. For those who haven't been through this, it's hard to understand how challenging it can be to face all these changes and choices after time in a system where everything stands still.

One of the biggest hurdles is finding an affordable place to live. Often, housing near halfway houses or in areas more prone to crime and drugs is all that's available. After coping with prison confinement, you're suddenly thrust back into the real world, where everything seems to come at you fast. Simple things like opening a bank account can feel like a monumental task, especially as you navigate the reactions of those around you. Being a felon is something you carry forward, and while some people are supportive, others may stigmatize you. I've found it helpful to bring it up myself on my terms, which often opens the door for others to share their experiences or those of loved ones. These shared stories remind us that incarceration touches more lives than we realize and helps reduce the stigma.

I've often thought about how powerful it would be if the entrepreneurial spirit I saw in so many women inside could be supported upon their release. Unfortunately, finding customers or support can be challenging when you cannot affiliate with others on parole. An incubator program designed for those starting over could be a tremendous help—offering a place to learn, share ideas, and gain support as they build new businesses. Imagine if we had resources beyond drug rehab, focused on practical business skills, mental health, and personal growth.

Where is the credit union that specializes in serving formerly incarcerated individuals? Access to service like business loans, insurance, and counseling could be life-changing. Many returning citizens face high risks and need a specific kind of compassionate and pragmatic support.

If the purpose of incarceration is rehabilitation, then we need more focused efforts on providing reentry support. Too often, it feels like a hamster wheel that's hard to get off, where society only addresses the symptoms, not the root causes.

Women's experiences in prison are often misrepresented, focusing on sensationalized stories that don't reflect reality. The number of women in prison has grown by 475% over the last 40 years, and this crisis affects people from all walks of life. If we genuinely want people to succeed and thrive upon release, we must invest in resources that help them break the cycle and stay motivated to build better lives.

Safe, clean, affordable housing is critical. But more than that, we need community acceptance. We need a shift from 'not in my backyard' attitudes to integration and support. Retired professionals could create incubators where women learn to operate businesses in a supportive environment, using empty shopping centers or community spaces. Car dealerships could offer fair prices and limited warranties to help women secure reliable transportation. We need practical programs for trauma recovery, parenting, technology, and vocational training, all tailored to the needs of those reentering society. This is not just a wish, but a pressing need for our communities.

Counseling is essential for learning how to move forward without constantly apologizing. Society doesn't yet understand that once someone has served their time, they deserve a real chance to rebuild without the lingering shadow of stigma.

Continuing education (CE) classes for those working within the judicial system are not just beneficial; they are necessary. Judges, attorneys, counselors, and educators could benefit from learning about all phases of the system. A more informed perspective could foster better communication and policies, reducing recidivism. This is not just a suggestion, but a crucial step towards a more just and effective system.

The prison process has three main phases. The first is the legal stage, where lawyers and courts manage your case, with decisions about bail and initial sentencing. If more of those involved in this stage understood what awaits in prison, they could better prepare individuals.

The second phase is prison life, where newcomers face a steep learning curve. The third phase involves moving to a halfway house and adjusting to probation. Smooth transitions between these stages can make a huge difference, yet many women enter each stage without guidance.

I was fortunate to have my family and home to return to, though I came out with more debt than ever. It was tempting for me to hide from the world rather than confront the many challenges ahead and over time, I've seen many women struggle because of a lack of support. What specific challenges do women face when reentering society after being incarcerated? What support and resources are available to help formerly incarcerated individuals start over and rebuild their lives?

We need to ask some serious questions and start looking for serious answers on how the reentry process may be improved to support individuals transitioning from incarceration to society? I've been out for over five years, and writing this book has been part of my healing process. I hope that it helps others understand this journey and inspires positive change.

THE END

ABOUT THE AUTHOR

Cheryl's journey had humble beginnings. She grew up poor in a struggling Hispanic immigrant family in Kansas City, Kansas, where she was the third eldest of 11 children. A former elementary school teacher who left behind the blackboard for the business world, and over the years, built a corporate empire encompassing twenty-two different businesses that showcase a wide range of personal interests and concerns. Cheryl became one of America's most successful female entrepreneurs, innovators, and business leaders.

Through hard work, determination, and a positive attitude, Cheryl exemplifies what is possible. Her motivational talks and mentoring programs inspire and empower people, particularly women, worldwide. Cheryl leads by example, showing others that anything is possible if they believe in themselves and are willing to work hard.

When she founded her first company in the basement of her home in 1982, Cheryl focused on succeeding in two male-dominated industries—trucking and insurance. A pioneer in the field of daycare in the workplace, she passionately believes in helping others to help themselves. She has received numerous awards and accolades for her accomplishments, which have garnered the attention of many local, national, and international publications.

Not one to retire, Cheryl now manages many business interests, including directing the efforts of a new business she founded to partner with and provide consulting and administrative services for a variety of start-up and growth companies. Cheryl has a history of generous support for many local organizations and enjoys personally mentoring budding young entrepreneurs.

Cheryl now has identified a new passion; as Founder of the non-profit Women of Worth, she draws on her personal experience within the US penal system to create awareness of the rapid growth of women entering the prison system. She refers to them as "invisible" because everything related to the penal system is male-oriented. She believes these women and their specific needs should be recognized. She isn't looking to overhaul the penal system but rather to bring much-needed attention to the particular needs a woman has while and after being incarcerated.

Beyond her professional life, Cheryl's passions include philanthropic work, developing and speaking about education on women in the penal system, property management and development, interior design, needlepoint, and reading. Above all, she treasures her family and is a proud wife and mother of two sons, and a daughter in-law. She also loves spending time with her two step-children and grandchildren.

RESOURCES

We're here to support you;

WEBSITES

Bureau of Prisons
www.bop.gov under "location" you can select the
Prison or Camp and learn how;
- Inmate Mail
- Inmate Money – Western Union & United States
  Postal Service
- Freight and non-USPS parcels
- Staff Mail
- Commissary Sheet & Prices
- Admissions and Orientation (A&O) Handbook

AARP (formerly known as American Association of
Retired Persons)
Medical Directive by State
www.aarp.org/caregiving/financial-legal/free-printable-
advance-directives

Eforms
Simple Last Will & Testament Template by State
www.eforms.com/wills

Limited (Special) Power of Attorney Form
www.eforms.com/power-of-attorney/limited

Women of Worth
Resources for former and incarcerated women
including the children's book;
Mommy Loves You Everywhere
www.womenofworthwow.org

Leading Women Enterprises
Providing Unique Services & Products for Women
within the US Penal System
www.leadingwomenenterprises.com

APPENDIX – TASK LIST

Chapter 22

ACKNOWLEDGMENTS

I would like to express my deepest gratitude to the incredible women with whom I shared my time while incarcerated. Your strength, resilience, and camaraderie made an indelible impact on me, and I carry those lessons forward with gratitude and humility. Together, we faced challenges that shaped us into stronger individuals, and I will always cherish the bonds we formed.

To my family, friends, team, and those who supported me during my absence, words cannot fully capture my appreciation. Your unwavering belief in me, your encouragement, and your efforts to keep my life moving forward while I was away were sources of strength. Your love and support anchored me through the darkest of times, and I am forever grateful for the role you played in my journey back.

For Speaking engagements or information contact Leading Women Enterprises, or the charity Women of Worth;

V. Cheryl Womack
PO Box 8042
Prairie Village KS 66208
Email: info@leadingwomenenterprises.com

Made in the USA
Columbia, SC
03 February 2025

52604706R00085